Bill Snelling

MOTORCYCLES, MATES
and MEMORIES

Recalling sixty years of fun in British motorcycle sport

T0386731

www.veloce.co.uk

First published in November 2020, reprinted February 2021 and 2024 by Veloce, an imprint of David and Charles Limited. Tel +44 (0)1305 260068 / e-mail info@veloce.co.uk / web www.veloce.co.uk.
ISBN: 978-1-787115-81-1

Bill Snelling

MOTORCYCLES, MATES and MEMORIES

Recalling sixty years of fun in British motorcycle sport

Contents

DEDICATION

This book is dedicated to Pat (the missus)
and
The Martin Ward of Ramsey & District
Cottage Hospital, Isle of Man

Introduction

The catalyst for this book came when I had an enforced ten-week hospital stay in 2019. A replacement hip had become infected, I was flown to Whiston Hospital, Liverpool, it was removed and then they airfreighted me, hipless, back to the Island, where I took up residence in the Martin Ward of Ramsey Cottage Hospital. The service from all departments there could not be faulted, the physio there even got me walking on crutches with one hip.

Only one thing rankled – some of the other patients! I was probably the youngest one in there, but you would have thought the actions of some were more akin to a 16-year-old on Viagra! Instead of a single nurse going to treat a patient, they had to go in mob-handed. I kept the alarm bell button handy, not for my own sake: one afternoon I heard a sound of a falling body from the toilet/shower room, I summoned assistance and the nurses went to the rescue of a chap who had slipped over in there. One patient must have thought he was in a hotel; three nights running at 3am he rang the bell and demanded (very loudly) to be served tea and toast!

There were stand-out gems as well, there was a gentleman who had been in the first wave of troops on to the Normandy Beach during WWII. He was awarded the Légion d'honneur by the French Government. He was a lovely, unassuming man and I was honoured to see the wonderful medal that had been presented to him at Government House, by the Lieutenant Governor. It is a pity the Manxmen who won such an honour (I believe there were around 14 of them) are not mentioned in the Wikipedia lists. The Manx should be there in their own right, not lumped in with the UK.

To keep my mind off the antics of the fondling ward mates I opened my computer and started to jot down some of my motorcycling memories, which form this book. My medical notes state: "Obsessed with the computer" – they didn't know what I was doing!

The book has brought me back in touch with many of my motorcycling mates from 50, 60 years ago, when I had hair, teeth and ability! Sadly, some have passed 'under the chequered flag' since those halcyon days.

Early days, down south

MY FIRST RIDE

1952

As far back as I can remember, our family transport was always a bike and sidecar. I recall that Dad removed the entire living room window from our house in Canterbury to get the Vincent in during a cold winter, to work on it. The first bike I was aware of was a Series C Vincent, attached to a double-adult sidecar. I can still recall the registration: HHR 451. We covered thousands of family miles on this machine; we were living in Kent at that time, and nearly always on holidays went down to Weymouth, where we met with other members of our family. According to my sister, I am 'alleged' to have nearly kicked the bottom out of the sidecar one day at Folkestone, because I was denied yet another candy floss!

1959

One year, Dad fancied a change, so we headed north and finished up in Ullapool on the west coast of Scotland. The wind was horrendous up there; they were even pegging the caravans down. After a day of this, we decamped to Fort William, where it rained all day. Fed up with the Scottish weather, we headed back down to Weymouth to rejoin the rest of the family. Approaching Carlisle, it was obvious that something was amiss with the outfit. The rear suspension unit had failed; the collar holding the spring under tension had come adrift. We found Tiffen's of Carlisle, a Velocette agent. Billy Tiffen had won the Scottish Six Days Trial in 1936 on a Velo KSS. His machine exists to this day and now resides here on the Island. They repaired the spring unit, and we then carried on down to Weymouth.

One year, we were riding down towards Pentewan Sands in Cornwall, near the Lost Gardens of Heligan, when the outfit slewed sideways; the sidecar mudguard had come adrift and was under the wheel. Another sidecar rider stopped and gave us assistance to get it bolted back in place.

Just recently, pics emerged on Facebook of HHR 451, being retrieved from a shed where it had lain for over 30 years. I was able to pass a picture of it to its new owners, festooned by yours truly, my sister and other youngsters at a camp site. Delighted it is in the hands of a Vincent enthusiast; I hope they keep the patina of the machine as it was all those years ago, Dad was never into polishing, a tradition I uphold to this day! I gather this bike has now found a new home in Belgium.

Dad was mistakenly seduced by the specification of the Ariel Square 4, so he went to George Clarke's and part-exchanged HHR for a Squariel: bad mistake! He hated it, and within the week went back to buy his beloved HHR 451 back – too late, it had gone. What they had for sale was a Series D Vincent, RGW 798, which Dad bought and then attached to a Watsonian Avon sidecar. This was a prototype that had been exhibited at Earl's Court: the chassis was made with oval tubing. The salesman indicated that RGW was a Lightning, with its black crankcases. When Dad realised it wasn't, George Clarke's amended the HP arrangement to reflect they had sold him just a Series D Shadow.

The first time Mum and Dad went out solo on the Vincent RGW 798, it was to visit Hugh and Eunice Evans at Biggin Hill. They stopped, but Dad didn't put any feet down, and they toppled over. Mum was heard to say, "You silly sod!" as they righted the bike.

When Dad passed on, RGW 798 was in pieces, and we sold it to Chas Guy of Conway Motors, shortly before he was killed at Goodwood. The bike is no longer registered on the UK vehicle database, so I guess the parts were used to keep other Vincent Series Ds on the road. The next owner of HHR 451, we found out later, lived in Thornton Heath, near Croydon, where Dad worked as a dental technician for many years. He always rode to work on a fixed-wheel pushbike, to be able to stop quick and pick up pieces, nuts, bolts, Triumph rocker box caps, whatever, on the road. One day, he came home with a Vincent footrest rubber. I wonder if it came off HHR 451?

Most Monday evenings the whole family would troop down to Wimbledon Speedway on Plough Lane to support the Dons. Those were the days when they had some speedway superstars: Ronnie Moore, Barry Briggs and Cyril Brine took on, and often beat, the likes of the Belle Vue Aces, headed by Peter Craven and the Norwich Stars, led by veteran Aub Lawson with Trevor Hedge and Ove Fundin. The stadium was always packed, from grannies to toddlers. It started my love of Castrol R!

1960

In 1960, I badgered Mum and Dad to take us over for the TT. I had been reading the Green 'Un (*Motor Cycling*) and the Blue 'Un (*The Motor Cycle*) for many years. We didn't have a phone at that time, so Dad looked in the *Motorcycle News* and wrote off, getting digs in Santon. It was my first sail; I recall the boats being crammed with bikes, and watching, fascinated, as they craned bikes, outfits and cars off at the Island. I had never seen the underside of Dad's Vincent before! We had the tank nearly drained dry at the Liverpool docks, so when we disembarked we asked a Douglas harbour policeman where we could get petrol. "Along the North Quay, you will see the Shell sign." We found it, a single pump inside a garage. You went in onto a turntable, fuelled up, it was then turned through

180 degrees and you left, but not before you were given a felt Castrol flag, and the Shell book of the 1959 TT. In later life, this was my first place of work on the Island, E B Christian's Lucas depot.

We were guided out to Santon and found our digs. This was a chalet adjoining the Murray's house. Charlie and Emily Murray were running a motorcycle museum and café from their Santon premises (the Murrays later moved it to Peel, then to The Bungalow on Snaefell before finally returning to Santon).

Dad had a bit of clutch trouble on the Island; and who should he see in Victoria Street, Douglas, but Tubby, who was the store man at Millars of Mitcham, our local Vincent dealer. He got the spares sent over and it was repaired while we were there.

Settling into the chalet, I could hear engines revving behind our accommodation. There was an oval track in the back garden, an old Rudge was being ridden round, and also a miniature speedway bike, called the Houghton Blaby, with a 98cc Villiers engine. It had been used as the mascot's bike for the Leicester Speedway team. "Would you like a ride?" asked Charlie Murray. I declined as I had never ridden a motorised machine in my life. "Course you can," said Charlie, and plonked me on the seat of the Blaby. "Twist that grip a little on the right hand bar, but not too much." I rode round that oval for quite a while, with Charlie in attendance, until we just about ran out of petrol. Dad came out with the camera and snapped my first ever ride. So, my motorcycle odyssey began at 13 years old, and still carries on to this day.

We went to Glen Helen. During the first race, the Ultra Lightweight TT, the third rider round slid to earth, at our feet – it was Mike Hailwood! Many people remember his falling at Sarah's Cottage in the 1965 Senior, on that day he restarted the MV to win, but in 1960 he was just a rising star. I was astounded, heroes weren't supposed to do things like that!

1962

A family friend, and my godfather, was Stan Lewis, from Maidstone. Stan raced a Mk VIII Velo KTT in the late '50s, and knew Arthur Lavington well. When I knew Stan in later life, his mounts were a Vincent Meteor 500, with 150,000 miles on the clock and still with its original primary chain, and a Mk I cammy Velo, known to all and sundry as 'the little rough un.' The paintwork was a little 'basic' and someone said to Stan, "I see you've tarmaced it, when you gonna roller it?"

By this time our family had moved to Mitcham, on the outskirts of South London. Arthur Lavington, after leaving the Velo dealer L Stevens of Goldhawk Road, was running a small Velo repair shop, first in Earlsfield and later in Tooting, where it was based in an old house and stables behind a bakery and a radio shop. Me and school had drifted apart, and I joined Arthur and his mechanic Roy Church when I was 15. My first job there was to take a clutch off a Venom, that is why I am completely au-fait with a Veloce clutch, not these strange ones with a central rod – they bemuse me! I was also the gopher, for bits that Arthur did not have in stock. My regular haunts were Elite Motors in Tooting, and Hughes of Tooting; Vern at Hughes hated us buying his Triumph BTH points for 'our' Velocettes. For Velo bits I was sent to A H Tooley at Burnt Ash Hill, London SE 12, Roy Smith Motors at Surbiton, and L Stevens of Goldhawk Road. All MOTs were done at MAC Motors in Colliers Wood, where old Mac would always reminisce about his old Velo, but very rarely did he ride or even touch the bike for testing; he relied on Arthur's expertise.

Arthur had the contract to service the Metropolitan Police fleet of LEs, and this kept us quite busy. We had an early morning visit by a pair of bobbies; they had been playing tag on night shift, and one had rear-ended the other, damaging the pannier on one by intimate contact with the legshield of the other! As we were sorting out the mess, we heard another Noddy arrive. It was the local sergeant who normally popped in most days for a cuppa. He didn't stop this day, he silently rode round us straightening the two bent bikes in the yard, and went back to the station. Nothing was ever said about this event. The LE was a pain in the arse to work on; the whole body had to come off to get to the clutch, if the bike was left for any length of time the plates used to rust together. A dodge was to scoot off, drop it into gear and ride around, putting the brakes on to free the rust. Trouble was, the Noddy brakes weren't that good! A cure was to drill a hole in the clutch housing, then you could prise apart the plates, or, when left over winter, simply hold in the clutch by tying back the clutch handlebar lever.

The points spring was not the best on the Miller generator; we used to get quite a few in that would only run mid-throttle. By putting more tension on the spring, it made a world of difference!

Issues with Lucas and BTH mags could sometime be put down to the point spring breaking and the points bouncing.

One Saturday, a cammy roared up the slope to Arthur's shop. Jeff Clew was Travelling Marshal at a Crystal Palace race meeting, but he had just broken the clutch cable at dinner time. He was able to fit a new one and be back in time for racing to proceed.

Whilst working at Arthur's, the Velo Owners Club was expanding, and I recall going to the inaugural meetings of the Reading Centre (Ben Mallinson, Geoff Cole etc), the Bristol Centre (Pete Isaacs, Phil Fetherstone), and the Manchester Centre (Bill Healy et al). Most times I would ride the Viceroy to these meetings.

In later years, Mum and Dad became the Velo Club's joint membership secretaries, and they often used to get Velo fellows staying for the odd day; even a French contingent once. I was constantly fed tea and buns whilst working in the garage at the bottom of the garden, late into the night: that probably explains my corpulent physique! Mum reckons Dad only bought the house because of the double garage. It housed a Singer Le Mans chassis in the roof; we advertised it free in *Motor Sport* and other car magazines, but there were no takers, so I think Dad cut it up and gradually introduced it into our, and our neighbours', dustbins over a few months.

For a Federation of One Make Motorcycle Clubs (what a mouthful, BMF rolls off the tongue so much better!) annual rally at Beaulieu, Arthur borrowed the Roarer and the Model O from Veloce to display. The Roarer was the supercharged racing twin built for the 1939 TT, to be ridden by Stanley Woods. He practised the machine but raced the more-proven single.

At that time we had it, the machine was a bare skeleton, with no innards. I know because we took the square plate off the side of the engine and peered in. Ivan Rhodes and family have re-manufactured all the internals, and it is a credit to them that it has covered many demonstration miles under their ownership.

Later, I enjoyed a very brief ride on the 1939 Model O, another Velo twin, but this one a road machine, Titch Allen owned it for a while, in partnership with John Griffith and Stanford Hall, home of their bike collections, and also the venue for many Velo Club rallies.

Arthur had a special LE which he and wife Brenda used to ride, and very often win, road trials in the South Eastern Centre. The engine of MLO 710 was standard, but it had a double-skinned rear frame. This enabled him to use Girling units, the standard Noddy just had spring units, no damping. On the front, he had a set of cut-down Venom fork springs to give it more ground clearance, it was easy to deck the footboards when cornering enthusiastically. One year, when Brenda was otherwise occupied, I rode as navigator with Arthur in one of Dorking MCC's Saturday Night and Sunday Morning road trials, which went from Surrey to Wales. In the middle of the night, we ran out of fuel, by a farm. There was an adjacent lorry, so we checked if it was petrol – it was, so we quietly siphoned a few pints to get us under way. As we were siphoning, we became aware that we were not alone – a collie was sitting alongside; it did not make a sound, so we gave it a pat and carried on. After finishing, we made our way home. Going down the High Wycombe bypass, now the M40, I realised our trajectory did not coincide with the radius of the road – Arthur had fallen asleep at the bars! A quick slap on the shoulders brought him to again. I also navigated Arthur on the Brighton semi-sporting trial, held in Sussex around the South Downs. The Noddy wasn't the ideal bike for this event; we were dropping down from Ditchling Beacon when the wheels dropped into a deep rut, deep enough for the wheels to lose contact with terra firma. On the footboards, we slid down that hill at a great rate of knots!

I only visited the Hall Green Veloce works once, with Arthur, and was quite shocked to see how such an antiquated set of buildings could produce such wonderful machines. The assembly line had been extended by knocking a hole in a wall, it was still in that parlous state after many years. They were also making parts for Shorrocks superchargers and taking on other engineering jobs for Birmingham firms.

Time makes me forget what bike I was learning on, but I had goosed it just before my driving test, so we put 'L' plates on Arthur's Mk I cammy, and I headed to Wimbledon, hoping the tester did not know it was a 'skinny' 350; he didn't and I got a pass.

THE FIRST DRAGON RALLY

I had taken to reading the Blue 'Un (and the Green 'Un) from an early age. In *The Motor Cycle*, late 1961, John Ebbrell had mooted the idea of a British winter Rally, based on the German Elephant Rally held at the Nürburgring. So in 1962 the Dragon Rally was born, which still runs to this day. I persuaded Dad that we had to attend; Mum declined to join us, so we set off early that January morning, with a trailer hitched on the bike filled with all the camping gear. There were no motorways in those days. I recall pulling into a lay-by near Birmingham where the Birmingham MCC had laid on a coffee stop for those heading for Bryn Bras Castle. Before we hit the site, Dad pulled into a small shop to buy breakfast supplies: eggs, bacon, etc. The shopkeeper was bemused by the amount he sold that day, no one had told him of the rally. Parking in the grounds on Bryn Bras, we signed in, collected our badge and got the tent erected. A big old Brough outfit pulled up alongside, ridden by an elderly chap, the sidecar disgorged a large number of youngsters. I didn't realise at the time it was 'Titch' Allen with his brood and friends. Later that evening, the call was made to assemble for the headlight parade, a ribbon of light that snaked its way round the Welsh countryside; I wonder if they still hold that these days?

Dad suffered from 'white finger' syndrome, probably caused from the vibrations from the v-twin. It only affected his right hand, so he used to stick it in his coat, and ride the outfit left-handed on the throttle – just try it!

We also attended the second Dragon Rally, this time at Gwrych Castle, near Abergele in Conwy. This was in a semi-derelict condition, but good enough for the Dragon, some people were bedded down in pigsties!

In 2015, Pat (the missus) and I were holidaying in Wales when we saw a sign to Bryn Bras; for memory's sake I had to go and see it. It is now holiday apartments, I wonder if the current owners knew about its Barbour-clad past!

In 1962, I took the coach to Blackpool airport and flew across for the Manx Grand Prix on a Bristol Super-freighter, the one where the nose opened and you drove in. I swear I don't know how that thing flew: it just went in a straight line and the earth curved away from it! I stayed at Mrs Morrison's, Peveril Street, Douglas, along with a couple of MGP riders, London Policeman John 'Noddy' Wheeler and Mick Miller, foreman of Roy Smith Motors, then of Surbiton. I recall hijacking the landlady's push bike to get to the pits, and also getting a right bollocking for riding across a Halt sign without stopping.

That year, I was roped in to be part of Joe Dunphy's signalling crew at the Gooseneck. My eyes were younger than the rest of the crew, so, with binoculars, my job was to pick out riders as they came out of the Waterworks, so the boys could plot Joe's progress. The vegetation has grown so much, you don't get that wonderful view these days of the riders sweeping round Tower Bends towards the Gooseneck. Joe won the Senior Manx that year.

Mick Miller later married Norma, the landlady's daughter. An ex-rider, now domiciled on the Island, once said: "We always left a girlfriend in the Isle of Man. It's nice to see everyone at TT and MGP time, but its nice to have a our quiet little Island again, when we can get our pubs, restaurants and girlfriends back!"

1963

MY FIRST TRIAL

Reg Ascott Trial, Dews Farm Pits, Middlesex, 10th March, 1963, just a month before I was 16. I was riding with Tony Clear on his 1930 Ariel Colt. It was not the most memorable start to a trials career judging by my results, but look who was riding that day, a veritable who's-who from the Southern section of the Vintage Club of the 1960s.

Later that year, I won the Novice award at Holtye Common, a hellish muddy venue, where I saw Sir Walter's 'bacon slicer', a Raleigh ridden by Ken Denman, manfully struggling through the Sussex gloop, but Mike Vangucci made it look easy on his Ariel.

At one of these events, Velocette historian and author Jeff Clew allowed me a run on his Model U Velo two-stroke trials machine, called 'Eustace.' Jeff had received (allegedly) a raw deal from AMC some years ago, he was praying to win the pools, so he could buy and burn Plumstead to the ground!

My 16th birthday was on April 11, 1963, it was a Brands Hatch race meeting day. My sister bravely loaned me her Lambretta Sports Scooter, the model with the abbreviated leg shields. Corker hat atop, I sallied forth using the route we had taken so many times as a family. Probably Mike Hailwood won a few races that day, chased by Derek Minter. Bill Ivy may have won the 50cc race, and Bill Boddice would have been harried by the scruffy ETY Triumph of Ted Young, and then it was homeward bound. Youthful enthusiasm got the better of me as I rode through Knatts Valley, where they used to hold hill climbs, because I went straight through a hedge, without any damage. Experience number 1, I hate to think what number I am up to now!

In my formative years, I owned a couple of Greeves and an AJS trials machine, so forgettable I can hardly remember them, I don't think I used them in trials.

During the winter of 1963-64, we got a call from one of Dad's old army dental corp friends. His son, who was also in the army, had to abandon his BSA B31 outfit near Sevenoaks as the clutch was slipping and he had to get back to camp. We got some drive back on the machine, I had never ridden a sidecar before, how hard could it be? We set off, going down past the Badgers Mount Café, there is a long sweeping left hander. The bike was twitching a little, so I gave the steering damper a tweak. Not known at the time, but the top fork nut was cracked, I was, in fact, crushing the head bearings whilst adjusting the damper. I turned that curve into a straight, and hit a Cortina just behind the front wheel and went over the roof. Dad was following on in his brand new Mini Countryman; he quickly got off the road onto the verge, but the wayward Cortina spun, then hit the car following Dad, which just happened to contain the father and brother of the chap whose outfit I was riding. So in one hit, I destroyed the family's total transport system. It was found that, at that time, my insurance as a 16-year-young whippersnapper did not allow me to ride any other vehicles, the upshot was a six-month ban, plus I had to pay for the Cortina in instalments.

When I was a member of the Wimbledon Dons MCC, I rode in a few trials on a 500T Norton, but not very successfully. I recall riding down to Goodwood one day, no vans or trailers then, you rode to an event and then rode home again, by gum it was hard event. On one section I came a right purler and thought I had split my head open; the oil tank cap had come off and I was being anointed by my own lubricant!

At an event on WD land near Aldershot, I tumbled again, resulting in a broken wrist (I was susceptible to those in my youth, I broke both in one day running up stairs and tripping). Ted Frend, former AMC works racer took me to the local hospital and then back. I didn't ride the bike home again that day!

One Friday night at the Wimbledon Motorcycle Club (a different club to the one I rode trials with), someone suggested we take a trip away for the weekend. Scurrying home to gather passports and toothbrushes, we departed and made our way from Dover to a nice hotel in the middle of the town of Bruges, where we dutifully drank our duty-free allocation on the first night, as you do. Touring the area, we found ourselves in the Dutch town of Sluis. We stopped at one the many restaurants and fancied the steak, mushroom and chips. This huge platter of mushrooms arrived; but where were the steaks? Inside the mountain of mushrooms! Fabulous food, with baskets full of chips, every time it went to just quarter-full, they whipped it away and brought another – what a challenge. We finally finished that course, but still had room for a sweet, a sundae containing just about everything they had in the kitchen. Cream, fruit, ice cream, some mighty alcohol (unknown variety but very nice), topped with a wafer and a sparkler. The sparkler slipped on mine as they were delivering it to the table, and the wafer caught alight! It was whipped away and replaced. After an hour or so, well satisfied, we headed for the town centre itself. A canal port with a long medieval history, Sluis was home to as many sex shops as you would want to look at! Pre-Euro, everything was priced in Francs, Deutschmarks and Gilders, plus Sterling. The boys were rubber-necking from the outside, so I thought to venture in, and they were right behind me! Whilst perusing the stock, someone wanted to pay by credit card, unusual in its day. The lad behind the counter had to ring the manager to get him to attend. A few minutes later, this chap rides in through the front door on a bicycle, parks it against a rack called 'Bizarre' (it really was), made the transaction, turned the bike round and rides out again: I swear 90% of the people in that shop never saw him arrive or depart! I thought it would make a wonderful Benny Hill-type sketch! We found the cyclist at many other sex shops, he probably ran them all, we didn't do any more perusing, when you've seen one ... etc.

There was hardly a Sunday went by that Velo fellows wouldn't drop by 3 Hadley Road, Mitcham, to chat, drink tea, and eat Mum's cakes. The 'soggy sponge' as I called it, was extremely popular, I now know it as a Victoria Sponge. Amongst them Pete and Beryl Redman were regulars, Pete and I would be fettling our bikes, Beryl was always a favourite of Mum and Dad, so she went to see them indoors whilst us boys were sorting out our Velo ailments. Once, when one of my mates started up to leave, we heard his bike's motor squeak, I remarked I hope it wasn't the back right barrel stud pulling out of the crankcase, this is shorter than the other three – it was!

Another time we were investigating a funny untraceable clicking noise coming from a friend's Viper, all the usual points were checked, without success, we spent days trying to trace it. We changed barrels, timing gears, anything to find it. It took many people, holding many bits in the engine, to trace that it was the timing side mainshaft loose in the flywheel! The drive-side shaft can work its way out of the fly wheel, a top-hatted shaft stops this gallop, but I have never heard of another loose timing side shaft – ever!

I remember leaving my sister's smallholding at Chawston, Bedfordshire, on my '54 MSS to come home to Mitcham. A funny vibration appeared, so I stopped to check the engine bolts were still tight, then rode the 70 miles home. Investigation showed that the drive side main bearing boss had fractured, this was beefed up for the Venom, which also had much lighter flywheels than the MSS. The motor had been rebuilt into Venom cases, although they looked in perfect nick, I changed all the timing gears, as I always had plenty of Velo bits lying round the garage!

I hardly ever made money out of bikes, I remember buying a '55 Velo MSS for a fiver, taking the manual BTH mag off, and selling it that same night for a fiver. What would all those Velos (about 15 in pieces) I had in the garage fetch these days? They could have made me a handsome pension – I wonder what they would have been worth now?

For most Southern riders, the Pioneer Run was the start of their motorcycling season, for Pete, Beryl and myself, we used to go into Kent and ride round the hop fields, I can still remember the smell of hops from when I was very young, a lot of our local community used to go down there to earn some dosh pulling the vines down and picking the hops.

The Velo Club started their St George Rally to rival the Dragon Rally. One year it was held near Peter Scott's Slimbridge nature conservation site. I am 'alleged' to have drunk most of a bottle of Southern Comfort that night, but memories of that evening are somewhat hazy! One lady guest was also a little worse for wear. That evening, there was a trio of us, one was holding to a tent pole, and leaning over at about 15 degrees angle, the others were holding on to him, also leaning over. The lass, who thought her horizon was a bit off centre, tried making conversation but kept falling over! I also recall a chair losing a leg, as the bowling alley that ran down the middle of the hall was being energetically used that night.

The next morning, I opened an eye. It didn't hurt, so I opened the other one, no problems. By this time Dad had breakfast sizzling in the frying pan. I enjoyed it, but fellow Velo lads were amazed considering my state the night before!

We joined Arthur Lavington's crew for TT 1963. My first actual mount to the TT was a Triumph Tigress scooter, the one with the 250cc four-stroke twin engine. Riding up the A49, the damn thing sheared a primary drive key at Whitchurch, luckily right outside a bike shop! Arthur took a very large bell tent to house his KTT in the paddock; imagine leaving your race bike unattended inside a tent these days!

Whilst there, a German sidecar racer had arrived late, and wanted a view of the circuit, so mate John Bashford offered to take him on a lap in his Venom outfit. I was always up for a lap, so joined him, along with Roger Boakes, both Sussex members of the VOC. All was well, John was behaving himself, until he got to Sulby Bridge. He must have been too enthusiastic, as the bike looped clean over the sidecar. We rushed right in, and John grabbed the exhaust pipe to lift it up. As we righted it, we were pleased to see just an irate German, not a squashed one! After a few minutes, we carried on at a slightly steadier pace. Approaching Creg ny Baa, the German was hammering on John's leg, and using the international 'slow down' signal. By the time we got back to the paddock, the German's team had prepared his BMW outfit ready for his (calmer) practice lap.

That damn primary drive key sheared on the last day we were on the Island, I was getting quite proficient at changing it by then. I took a gentle ride back home, and sold it the next day.

For the 1963 Blue Lamp Road Trial, run by the Metropolitan Police MCC, I navigated for BMW club member Herbert Kennard. One of Herbert's claims to fame (for me, anyway) was that he at one point employed Mandy Rice Davies as a housekeeper. The event started from New Scotland Yard. It was a very comfortable ride, but it rained all day; the speedo on the R60 laid virtually horizontal, and I had to continually ask Herbert to wipe the speedo to see the tenths of a mile. In road trials you have a route card and are asked to ride at a set speed, usually 24mph, which works out at a mile every two and a half minutes, four tenths of a mile in a minute. Secret checkpoints were dotted along the course to catch those who were either running too fast or too slow. To my amazement, we won; the trophy was a facsimile of the Blue Lamp seen at the start of every edition of Jack Warner's BBC police drama of the '50s and '60s. Herbert was out of the country on prize-giving day, so I collected the trophy on his behalf from Raymond Baxter at the Metropolitan Police Motor Club's annual dinner.

I rode many South-Eastern Centre road trials, and for a few years myself and Saltbox members Hugh and Eunice Evans teamed up to win the odd team prize, we were called 'Hugh and I.'

1964

For 1964 we were still scooter mounted at the TT, but a Velocette Viceroy this time. It seized at one point, and, would you believe, Quayside Engineering, South Quay, Douglas had new Viceroy pistons in stock, even though there may have been just two of these scoots on the Island; their stock could probably have gone back to the Model T Ford. When we put the engine together, we ran it without the huge silencer, and it sounded just like a Scott.

I rode many road trials on the Viceroy, mainly alone, but on one trial out Essex way I co-opted Jonathan Hill as navigator. The scoot did not have a trip on the speedometer, which made accurate time-keeping not easy, so it was my practice to drop it onto the footboard and spin the back wheel to an accurate mile. That day, I had forgotten I had a passenger, and pitched Jonathan onto the roadside! At another check, we must have ridden quite a way with a collie attached to Jon's boot, it was not a bike-friendly pooch!

My first vertical twin was a Triumph TR6, which had been built at Meriden to Police Saint spec, with racing inlet camshaft, standard exhaust cam, and a huge silencer. You could whack it through town centres at an indecent speed, with just a whisper. It had incredible acceleration. The licence plate was 680 CYR, from memory. I was riding home one night, with no goggles, when a bee hit me in the eye, both eyes watered, and I clipped the kerb and slid off. There was a small hole in my trousers, but a huge, steak-sized scab on my bum for a few weeks!

Dad and I bought a Moto Guzzi Zigolo, the 110cc version, with its pressed steel frame and horizontal two-stroke engine. It was a beauty, the handling was superb, and it went like stink for a little 'un. It was later passed on to Mike Vangucci. Some years later I was back living in the Island when I saw one, and recognised it as my old one – an engine side panel screw had disappeared while I was riding it, and I'd replaced it with another from a Honda.

When I was not riding myself, my normal road trial pilot was Derrick Blake, whose Venom reg was FKT – when it got bogged down on a semi-sporting trial somewhere near Dorking, you can guess what he called it! Derrick was later to become the Editor of *Fishtail*, the Velocette Owners' club magazine, I was Technical Editor at that time.

Pete and Beryl Redman, together with yours truly, squeezed into Pete's Reliant one evening in 1969, and we trundled off to Dawlish Warren, Devon, in search of a rigid MAC. It was an honest machine, at the right price, so we bought it, and dismantled it enough to take up the extra space left in Tamworth's 'plastic pig,' and headed back on the 190-mile journey home: it was walking pace at roundabouts, as the roof rack was also full of Velo! We stopped at the Yeovilton

Café on the way, which I remember was one of the checkpoints on the MCC Exeter Trial in the 1960s. When we got it home, the bike was all there, but the clutch was off. I had enough bits to sort it out, but we just could not get it right. We then found we were trying to reassemble with two MAC 7-plate thrust pins and one 9-plate Venom one: that ain't gonna work! That's the problem of having so many Velo bits of different models in boxes around the garage.

Over the years, my family had an eclectic array of cars. Dad always drove: I didn't have a car licence until I got to the Isle of Man. His fleet included a Riley 2.6 ex-police car, through Heinkel, to a 325cc Berkeley three-wheeler that loved being revved out, but sooted plugs if not driven hard. When I started racing in 1971 we bought the ubiquitous Thames 10-12cwt van. The gear change, with its myriad of rods and links, was a sloppy mess; in fact, I had the knack of changing gear more easily from the passenger seat when we went racing.

1965-1972

In 1965, during TT week, the Conister MC & SC ran a road trial. It started from the Rugby Ground by Quarter Bridge, and the route turned right at the Jubilee Oak at Braddan Bridge. As we passed, they were pulling two corpses out of what is now Joey Dunlop House, two guys had come off the boat, straight on at Braddan and into the front window of the house at a mighty speed. Some things never change.

The trial that year took us round many back roads which are now very familiar to me. Arthur Lavington won, I think Bob Currie from *The Motor Cycle* was second, and I finished fourth, winning £4 and a trophy.

I was a member of the Dorking Centre of the Velocette Owners' Club from 1963 to 1970, whose meetings were in those days held at the Hand in Hand, Boxhill, a venue shared (on different nights) with the Vincent Owners' Club. It was a nice run down the Sutton bypass, then across Walton Heath.

I also attended the North Kent Centre meetings at The Ship Inn in Strood. Opposite the pub was the training ship Arethusa, built in 1849, the last British warship to go into battle under sail. On outings to Rochester the boys introduced me to Chinese food: sweet and sour chicken and the like. On one occasion I had sold a Villiers 2T engine to one of the members, and to get it down there it was lashed to the rear of the saddle of the Viceroy. Boy, that was a hairy ride! Other times we would ride out to The Yew Tree, Doddington. The landlord was a good friend of most of the boys, and lock-ins were popular, so it was sometimes a very late ride home!

In 1966 the Velo Club held its annual rally at Place Manor Hotel, in St Anthony in Roseland, Cornwall, and I rode there with Pete and Beryl Redman. Pete remembers the sound of the two Velos booming their way up the hill out of Mevagissey on the ride down. That was my first meeting with 'Skid' and Fran Rowe, who also later emigrated to Mona's Isle, as well as many others from the Devon and Cornwall VOC, some of whom, sadly, have have passed 'under the chequered flag.' It was the first time I'd tasted cauliflower cheese, apparently they were a bit short of the green stuff so someone had hopped off and 'borrowed' some from a local farm (they grow a lot of it down there, so they probably didn't miss it!)

One evening, while we were staying at Place Manor, we had ridden back to Gerrans, the local pub, about eight miles away. The local ale was good, and so were the pickled eggs, and I consumed quite a lot of both! I was last to leave the pub because someone had hidden my helmet, but was first back at the hotel! There were tales of the local farmers leaving gates open at corners when the the bikes were around, just to be on the safe side!

Roseland is a promontory opposite Falmouth, and beautiful biking country. Velo club members Jack and Joyce Goodchild lived down there, and we stayed in their barn after the Land's End Trial a few times.

One year I wasn't riding in the trial, but went down on the Viceroy, the flat-twin two-stroke Velo scooter. Its 12-volt lights were a revelation, and going up a misty Porlock, I had a queue of six-volters tagged on. It was a bit misty, and when a 90-degree corner came up, followed by another, and then a third, I then realised I had ridden into a car park!

We were sitting outside The White Cottage, Portscatho, the Goodchild's family home, when a bike went past the end of the road. I was certain it was a GTP, so hared after it and stopped him. It was indeed a GTP, the old fella, Bill Lobb, lived locally, but he and the Goodchilds had never met.

In 2017 Pat and I went back to Roseland, Place Manor is a now a country estate and 'private – out of bounds' but the views across the Fal and from the Roseland headlands are still brilliant. We even managed to find the Goodchild's White Cottage, looking exactly like it did over 50 years ago.

ARTHUR LAVINGTON

Arthur Lavington had been for years the workshop foreman at L Stevens, the Goldhawk Road Velo dealers, alongside Geoff Dodkin, who also went on to start his own Velo business. Arthur rode the TT for many years. His first Island race was the 1949 Junior Clubman on a KSS. However, his Island baptism came to an abrupt end when the front fork spring broke at Hillberry. After that he competed on his Mk VIII KTT from 1954. In the early years he used the standard girder forks, but from 1960 he fitted it with Velo teles. Even though his KTT was basically a prewar machine, Arthur was rarely last in the Junior TT.

He also rode a Thruxton in the inaugural Production TT of 1967; it was fitted with triangular tyres, which Arthur never got on with, and he pulled in to retire after the first lap.

Arthur was practising for the 1969 Junior TT, when he was involved in an accident at Alpine Cottage, just before Ballaugh Bridge. It was deemed a racing accident. A much faster competitor (Mick Andrews) came up behind Arthur through the sweeps after Bishopscourt, and collided with him, pushing him across into the wall of the house that gave the corner its name. Arthur died the next day from his injuries.

After Arthur's passing, I was offered the entire business (except his Mk VIII KTT) for £5000. Dad prevaricated about spending that much money (1969), and BMG of Ilford snuck in and bought it. Pete Redman was lurking around Upper Tooting recently, and found that Arthur's workshop was still standing, the stables used as garages had gone, and it is now a secondhand car showroom and car wash facility. Probably the ivy is holding the old place up!

One year whilst on holiday on the Island, through a contact of Arthur's I bought a Mk I cammy Velo from a chap in Castletown. Knowing what I now know of the vendor's reputation, I wonder whose machine I bought!

WORKING LIFE

I was no longer working for Arthur at the time of his accident, I had moved to be a 'grease monkey' at the Shirley Service Station, on the outskirts of Croydon. It was an RAC accredited breakdown service, and I was sent out on the bike on more than one occasion to supply fuel and even fit a fan belt. This lasted about a year, then I moved to Geoff Dodkin's Velo emporium at Upper Richmond Road, East Sheen. I started there on the spanners, but gravitated to the spares side of the business, where I came into contact with many Velo owners, some of whom are still friends to this day.

One French chap brought in a Venom to be 'Thruxtonised.' It looked really sweet after all the work, but before he went back across the Channel he was grubbing in the gutter and smearing muck all over the new fairing, tank and everywhere, he wanted to make it look as rough as it was when it arrived so he wouldn't have to pay duty on the new bits when he went home!

Another chap came in and demanded the same rear mudguard stay for the Thruxton as shown in the Veloce catalogue; this was an artist's study, they changed the design for production. He could not be persuaded otherwise, I think he only received satisfaction when he received a letter from Veloce who pointed out the error.

When chatting about clutch parts, you always asked if the clutch thrust race was good, "Oh yes, the grooves are fine," they would reply. I then had to show them that there should be no grooves; the recent modification to use rollers instead of balls sorted out most of those issues.

We had customers from all walks of life; one local was the actor Anthony Valentine, who had a clubman-type Viper. He played the German Major Mohn in *Colditz* on the BBC, the scar on his face was real, caused by goggles hitting a kerb! He used to bring his latest flame through door, have a chat and leave by the back door, where we were signing how many points that one was worth.

Another actor arrived one day, Willoughby Goddard, who played Lamburger Gessler, in *The Adventures of William Tell* on TV. He was in with a cousin; Willoughby was a big lad, we had to open both doors to get him in. The playwright Robert Bolt bought a Honda Monkey bike from Geoff, his wife the actress Sarah Miles came in with the paperwork.

Geoff sold mainly Honda C50/70/90 scoots, as well as the Velo bikes and bits. When Kawasaki first came into the country, Agrati Sales of Nottingham were the importers. Geoff bought a 250 (Samurai) and 350 (Avenger), both two-stroke twins. By gum they were quick compared to what I was used to.

He also managed to purchase the last batch of Indian Velos that were assembled in America. Floyd Clymer was the man responsible for this project, having purchased the Indian trademark. Clymer had been the inaugural winner of the Pike's Peak hillclimb on an (American) Excelsior in 1916.

Geoff was never happier than after Mrs Dodkin Mk II appeared. Desne was a lovely lass; a Brummie, she had previously worked at Veloce, so was able to point Geoff in the direction of Veloce's suppliers of valves, gears, silencers, brakes, tanks, etc. This was about the time that Hall Green was closing down. Ralph Seymour's of Thame was also making Velo bits and pieces, and as it would have been pointless for both of us to be making the same bits, we set up a contra deal, and helped each other out. Seymour's produced the K119 union that fitted to the top of the timing cover to take oil to the rocker box. I also used to fit one in the rocker box, to save wear on the rocker box thread: a 90-degree petrol union, a small piece of rubber pipe, and away you go. It was a nice ride out to Thame, Oxfordshire. The property was an old fire station, where machines had to be hoisted up to the workshop on the first floor. It was good to bounce Velo part numbers with Liz Seymour, she really knew her stuff.

THE SALTBOX MCC
Pete and Beryl Redman, a Velo owning couple of friends, were members of the Saltbox MCC, based at the Saltbox Café, Biggin Hill, and they persuaded me to join in 1965. Normally you go from coffee bar to owners' clubs, I went the other way round. The 'Box had been the former Mess Hall for RAF Biggin Hill, a WWII fighter airfield, one of many fighter airfields that were dotted around the Kent countryside. The owner of the café, Bernie Britton, decided to start a club for his many motorcycling customers in 1961. The first event the newly formed Saltbox MCC held was a run to give blood to Bromley hospital; Bernie knew the value of good publicity.

In was in my Saltbox days that I grew to appreciate Bob Dylan and his music, I went with Pete, Beryl and Chris Bryant to the infamous 1966 Royal Albert Hall when he went 'electric' in the UK for the first time. We wore out 'Like a Rolling Stone' on the Saltbox jukebox.

The Saltbox Club ran trials, using a trial site just below the 'Box. We were setting out the sections one day, and my mount on that occasion was the Velocette Viceroy scoot, an opposed-twin two-stroke, not your regular trials machine. As expected, I got it stuck down a hole. Being a reed-valve two-stroke, the damn thing had the ability to run backwards: by switching the ignition off and on again, just as it stopped, it ran in reverse. So I gave it a big handful and rocketed out of the hole, just as Del Whitton and Bob Wilkinson were coming to rescue me, and they ended up pinned to the ground under the scoot! They were unhurt, just surprised to see a two-wheeler hurtling in reverse towards them.

One evening, a group of us took the Underground to the furthest point south. Someone drew a straight line back to the 'Box, and we followed the best we could on foot. This included climbing over the fence into Brands Hatch, along the start-finish straight, and out again. By gum, I was jiggered at the end of it, I think I fell off twice going home that morning, the hairpin at Crown Ash Lane and the roundabout below Addington.

At the hairpin on Crown Ash Lane, there was a footpath that went up through a wooded area towards New Addington; after the 'Box closed for the evening, we sometimes used to ride up there and sit chatting. Brian 'Stones' Sprawson arrived one evening, and said that a noddy-riding policeman was trying to get up, I guess we should not have been there on bikes. "He's not getting very far," said Stones, who had blasted past him at usual Stones pace, and possibly given him an elbow as well. Another time, we were sitting there when a figure appeared, somewhat worse for wear, he must have drunk a lot of wobbly beer that night. As he came close, we all started up and revved, his wobbly legs took him away at great speed, bouncing off the trees as he made his way home!

Off-roaders aways took the opportunity to arrive at the Saltbox via Crown Ash Hill, which ran from Oakwoods Lane up to the 'Box.

For years the Café occupied the original WWII wooden building, part of RAF Biggin Hill. Later Bernie built a substantial building round it, whilst still running the old Saltbox Café inside the shell, before knocking the original down. That building has since been demolished, and a set of 'Hobbit' houses has been built into the bank.

Just a half mile away was the Nightingale Café, which seemed to attract a different type of biker; more your average rocker type. We had them at the 'Box too, but being a motorcycle club, they were a rare breed!

The 'Box attracted motorcyclists of all genres. As well as 'coffee bar' racers, there were real racers such as Rex Butcher, Paul Coombs, Brian 'Stones' Sprawson and John Robinson, who passengered Swiss ace Fritz Scheidegger to TT, GP and world champion success – Fritz and John were Club Presidents. It was on our way back from the Land's End Trial in 1967, that we heard on a radio of the accident at Mallory Park that claimed the life of Fritz.

Paul Coombs constructed his own frames for his CRD (Coombs Racing Development) Triumph-powered machines. He sent the invoices for the tube to the licensing authority to get the machines registered. He very soon got a visit from a very hot and bothered chap from the licensing department, they had mistaken CDT (cold drawn tube) for conduit! I could suggest a few 'Box members who would have made a frame from that, but not Paul!

I got members Del Whitton and Pete Winchester interested in riding the

MCC trials. Del had ridden the events before on a Bantam, but when I knew him he had a cobby BSA A7 500 twin in ISDT spec, and Pete had a 500T Norton.

In 1966, the 'Box went camping down at Lynton in Devon. The Land's End trial that year finished at Newquay, so after that Del and I made our way back across country. At one point, I think Del fell asleep on the bike, because he rode up a bank and down again. We stopped for a rest, laid down in a forest and were soon dozing, only woken by a sharp shower of rain. Refreshed, we got back to Lynton.

It was Easter, plenty of people around, and the 'Box decided to walk down to nearby Lynmouth in search of scrumpy. We found it, we drank it, in fact we drank Lynmouth scrumpy dry that night! One of our group had a Land Rover, and was running round collecting members from the various hostelries. His Rover clipped a car that was pulling out of a car parking space. When we opened the car door, this geezer had also been helping to drink Lynmouth dry. He got out of his car, with assistance, we walked him round his car twice, then showed him the non-scratched side. We put him back in the driving seat, but hid his the ignition keys in the glove compartment.

Bernie instituted a series of fines throughout the year, it cost you a few bob for speeding etc, a bit more if you had an accident. During December, he would visit a local cash-and-carry wholesaler, barter a good deal and buy a van load of produce, which we then boxed up and delivered to the pensioners in Biggin Hill. Just think, if I lived in Biggin Hill, I would qualify for one of these now!

When the 'Box closed for the evening, the South Londoners used to go to the sausage sandwich and pie stall at Thornton Heath Pond. If I was on petrol duty at the Shirley Service Station, someone would drop me off a sausage sandwich, which I reheated by laying the electric fire on its back and using it as a toaster, we never burnt the place down!

If there was any dispute about whose was the quickest, Norton quicker than Triumph etc, it was often settled by a trip down to the Gatwick bypass: in those days you could really let it rip down there. One of our mates, Mick Tench had a Q-ship, it looked like a standard Trophy, but he knew how to put the Triumph together, many a café racer was humbled by this unassuming rocket ship; Mick always rode upright, with his head cocked to one side, as if listening to the engine.

For the TT, the 'Box stayed at 'Injebreck' with the Christian family – a boarding house on Woodbourne Road, near to the top of Bray Hill. They had stayed there for many years, and I joined the motley crew in 1967. After we arrived, tea and cakes were served. I was just about to put the sugar in, but it looked a little granular – it turned out to be salt. At about the same time, we heard a bang and an 'Ooh!' from the kitchen, where landlady Joan was smoking the exploding fag that one of the guys had given her – that set the scene for the whole holiday, a running battle between the household and the 'Box.

We would come back after wandering around Douglas in the evening, one night we found everybody's night attire machine-sewn together, another night I jumped into bed and nearly broke my ankle on the family bible they had put there. Realistic rubber snakes were also one of their ploys. There were always cheese sandwiches waiting in our bedrooms. The early ones home used to nick our sarnies, but that was stopped when we laced them with tabasco sauce!

We got up to all sorts of mischief there; one night, we swapped the living and dining rooms around, there would be bikes dragged indoors, total mayhem, but given in equal measure by our hosts. Joan's daughter Jill married her long-time boyfriend Peter Warriner, and Joan's granddaughter Jo was for many years a scrutineer at the TT/MGP.

One particular evening, we filled balloons with talcum powder and spread dried peas outside the family's rooms. The balloons were popped, Joan thought the electricity supply had failed, until she smelt the talcum powder and felt the dried peas under her feet. "All right guys, you win," was her observation. The water system at Injebreck was a bit antiquated, if you emptied a sink the water would make a 'dugger-dugger' noise going down. One night we filled all the sinks; at a cough we all pulled the plugs out, it was surprising that the resonance never brought the house down! We would probably be called vandals these days, but back then it was high spirits, given and taken in equal measure.

For the TT period, the Christian family was dispersed into various cupboards and cubby holes, as we took over the whole house, one son was even sleeping in the bath!

It's surprising how many came to their first TT on Tritons etc, but came back on Greeves the second time! We used to hunt out all the byways and green lanes.

As we were enjoying the crab baps down on Port Erin harbourside one day, someone noticed Pete Winchester's 500T Norton had a slight weep from the tank, and pointed it out, touching a battery lead, which sparked and set the tank alight. It was quickly removed from the bike and covered in a layer of sand from the beach. After an hour or so, maybe a few more crab baps later, we unearthed the tank, replaced it on the bike and rode home.

A couple of us had taken fishing gear, and we fished off the rocks behind the Marine Biological Station. I thought my line had snagged something, it was hellish heavy to reel in, and then a head broke surface: I had hooked an eel! A very long eel, something like a five footer. It was landed, but what to do with it? 'Stones' provided the solution by whacking it on the head until it looked like a skate. We strapped in behind the seat and took it back to the landlady's cat, it could still be munching through that monster to this day.

One year, we were going to watch practice at Windy Corner, going up the track via Glen Roy. We met an American couple, sitting at the bottom with their Harley Davidson. He was thinking about leaving it there and walking up to Windy Corner, so I suggested he take the Flintstone (my own mount, see Chapter 5), put it in first gear and it would find its way there. So it was me, his big missus and a Harley. I had never ridden any of the Milwaukee marvels, the low-down torque was a great asset for green-laning. She gripped on tight to me (holding about two stone of me plus Barbour jacket in both hands), and away we went. She was fascinated by the countryside as we rode higher, but kept turning in the saddle, which meant parts of me got turned, whether I wanted to or not. We got up without a hitch, but she was now gripping about three stone in each hand, and I had lost all my wrinkles! I have never ridden a Harley Davidson since, in fact my motorcycling heritage is lacking in a lot of modern rocket ships, no LC Yams, Honda Fireblades, Suzuki GSXs or the like. That was 30-odd years ago, before they put the stones down on the track to prevent erosion. I have been up there on a Honda C90 since the rock-strewn 'improvements' – standing on the rear footrests, I managed it with three dabs, but left a large lump of leg shield on one particular rock.

I never used to like leaving the Island, and would ride round on the final evening until very late at night.

I am still in touch with members of the 'Box from my days through Facebook; 95% of this world-wide media is garbage, but the 5% for motorcycling is golden!

In 1969, I took Dad's then solo Vincent to the Island for my annual holiday; he reckoned it always went better after I used it, a touch of 'decoking' I guess. Me and my 'Box companions were 'soft' trail riding around the Staarvey area, and were making our way over the top to Tynwald Mills. I lost grip and the bike went down, trapping my foot under the petrol tank. We both slid for quite a way, there was no damage to me, but the primary chain case had a few witness marks on it, though Dad didn't seem to notice.

I attended the 1970 Thruxton 500 Mile Production race, where I was most impressed by the Mead and Tomkinson BSA B50s. One developed an ignition fault and was pushed into the pits, and I could see the entire ignition system was mounted on a triangular plate; they just had to remove the plug lead, a jack plug and three Dzus fasteners. In less than a minute it was replaced and they were on their way again. It was also the first meeting where I saw Barry Sheene ride, he was on the Read of Leytonstone Kawasaki 500 triple, until it tossed him off and wiped its ignition system as it went down the road on its side.

1972

In 1972, The Vincent Owners' club ran high-speed trial and race meetings at Cadwell Park. That year they ran a 100-miler. I was still racing the Viper. It was my first meeting at Cadwell, but I got some knowledge of the course from Hugh and Eunice Evans, and Ray Knight. Getting there early on Friday, I walked the circuit to get some familiarisation. The 100-miler was the first event of the day, with a mixture of road-going solos and Vintage machines. It was an event where you were passing and being passed throughout the 67 laps of the Club circuit. I recall being passed on the Park Straight by a Bonneville, and passing a 500 Triumph at the same time. There appeared to be communication between these riders, only later did I find it was John Musson on the Bonneville (who won the race) and his wife Hilary. I was also entered in the 500cc races later that day. The weather was patchy, rain showers on and off. In the first race, I found myself dicing with Malcolm Elgar on a 500 Egli Vincent. The Viper was supposed to red-line at 7000, but I was taking it to 8000 to get it out of the hairpin (it was fitted with W&S coil valve springs). I got beat into second place by half a wheel. Another bacon bap (or three) were consumed, then it was time for the second 500 race. Carrying the excess weight of a short portly figure and all those bacon baps was a handicap to a clutch start, so I was always playing catch-up. On the first lap I came round the Gooseneck with three Velo (500s) in line across the track; I overtook them on the grass, and chased after the Egli and Malcolm Elgar. The rain came down even harder but I was catching him up. Being of slight build (him, not me), his Egli Comet was moving around a lot on the damp track, going round Chris Curve on the last lap, every time he wound it on, it slid; with 17 stone chubbily sitting on a 350, mine held its line and I passed him going into the Gooseneck, I could hear him coming at Mansfield, but held on to win by less than half a wheel, my only race win! That's why Cadwell Park holds a special memory for me.

At the Rally of a Thousand Bikes at Mallory in 2010, what should be on the Bonham's stand in advance of an auction, but the very Egli Comet I had diced with all those years ago. Those high-speed trial meetings were great fun, it was a half-hour blast instead of a 5-lap scratch, and I am sure they helped my riding ability.

Later in 1972, I joined a good group of riders that were staying at the Ainsdale, Empress Drive, Douglas. Ray Knight, Roger Bowler, Hugh and Eunice Evans, Alan Walsh and Ron Baylie were residents for TT '72.

Roger Bowler was riding Ron May's Triumph Daytona. Ron was known to the motorcycling public as the grumpy ol' bugger from the workshops at the Tooting branch of Hughes of Wallington (as opposed to Vern, the grumpy ol' bugger in the stores!), but I shared a room with him, he had a keen sense of humour. In addition to the Daytona, Ron brought along his supercharged 3T Triumph sprinter, on which he held British sprint records. One day, before the Ramsey Sprint, he was idling it on the road outside the digs; a few guys passing were making comments, I knew what was about to happen, he hooked into gear, took it to the rev limiter, and disappeared up the road on the back wheel – no helmet, just his trademark black beret! The sheer sound nearly knocked the guys flat! We could hear him on Victoria Road, before calmly riding back and parking it in the garage. Roger Bowler's ride ended when he came back into the pits, with half a Triumph conrod in his helmet, he really knew how to blow a machine!

Alan Walsh was making his TT debut that year, riding his Trident in the Production and Formula 750 races. He had fitted green race brake linings to his four-leading-shoe front brake. Pitting in the Production race, he squeezed it a tad too hard and fell off in the pit lane. He finished the Formula 750 race, but there was a certain amount of greenery attached to the Trident when he came in. Last lap, he had got Signpost Corner wrong, and rode up the bank to join the spectators. The marshals and police rescued both bike and rider, assembled them in the correct order and said: "You'll finish, lad."

MY FIRST STINT ON THE ISLAND

I was due to go to the TT in 1975, and, I was getting a little jaded at Geoff Dodkin's, so I jacked the job in and went across to the TT; I said to Mum and Dad that I might stay on after the races. It was my tradition to head for the Friday midnight boat, then try and get some shut eye in the lower lounge of the Steam Packet ro-ro Manx Maid, where they allowed you to stretch out. It was straight up to see the early morning practice, which meant you were really buggered after a night and day like that, but it seemed to be worth it at the time.

After a fortnight's B&B, I moved into Trevor Hatton's spare tent. Trevor, a former Velo club member of the North Kent Centre VOC, was living in the tent all year. He did move into a flat in winter, but erected the tent in there too! Even the postman delivered our mail to 'The Blue Tent' and the 'Green Tent,' Tromode Road, he would unzip, throw the mail in and depart, nothing was ever taken in those days. I decided to stay, and looked round for a job, being taken on at the E B Christian Lucas depot on the North Quay, Douglas. We were all given green Lucas warehouse coats to wear, and were known to our customers as the 'Kermits.'

One branch of the Christian family empire was the main Ford dealer for the Island. Ken Blackburn, head Ford salesman, was a biker through and through; in his early days he had a GTP Velo and always fancied another. I found him a basket case, but it was in Birmingham. Fortuitously, there was a motor show in Birmingham coming up. Ken attended, with Norman Christian, son of the founder and, by then, head of the firm. Whilst in Brum, Ken nipped off and purchased the GTP, getting a local haulier to bring it back at their convenience at the right price. Norman Christian had been a top-class trials rider in his day, as was his brother David, but they were both eclipsed by the salesman from their Ballasalla Airport depot – Doug Crennell, who led the 1950 Scottish Six Days Trial on the first day.

I then found myself a small single room, with a single gas ring, and lived there for some months. I contacted my parents and asked for a suitcase of clothes, and, by the way, could they bring me up the racers? I got a day-trip ticket and Dad drove to Liverpool to meet the boat with the Velo Metisse, Thruxton and suitcases.

I later moved into a bungalow on the Murray estate at Santon; the Murrays had used these as holiday homes, and it had been the venue for our first holiday accommodation in the Island in 1960. The Murray family had come from Atherstone, Warks, where they had run a general hardware shop. Charlie was very much into his old bikes, and this was at a time when you could buy vintage and veteran machines from a few coppers to about five pounds. When they decided to emigrate to the Island, they bought the place in Santon, which had a café that fronted the Douglas to Castletown road. By this time Charlie had accumulated a vast amount of machines and spares, but how to move them? The solution was to buy a selection of nearly time-expired furniture vans (dirt cheap), fill them full and make their last journey across the sea. For many years the rotting relics were sitting behind the myriad sheds which housed his collection/museum. The latter took over a church hall in Peel, but later moved to the TSR tracking station at The Bungalow. I used to go up and assist Peter Murray when the museum was open, most winters a group of us would go and rearrange the exhibits, some years we would group marques, others we would put them in chronological order. They also had some wonderful Polyphons, one of which played 'I'll take you home again, Kathleen' – a beautiful tune. Mrs Murray, 'Em' as she was known, ran the tea room, with Mrs Teare, who lived at the adjacent house in Santon.

TV reception was very poor in the Santon area at that time, one Sunday we were trying to watch an old black and white film. Whilst Charlie was out of the room, some one switched the colour down, which made for better viewing, but after the end of the film Charlie said, "Reception is so bad, all I can get is black and white." We restored the colour balance when he left the room again!

I stayed on the Island for 18 months, but did not fully settle at that time, and I only had my TT friends there.

Motorcycle Sport magazine and despatch riding

MOTORCYCLE SPORT MAGAZINE

I returned to mainland UK (the 'adjacent island' as the Manx call it!) in 1976, and was looking for employment. I saw an advertisement for the position of ad man for *Motorcycle Sport* magazine (the original version, not the current Morton's version) and managed to get the job; I was aged 29 by then. Two illustrious predecessors in this job were Vintage Club stalwart Phil Heath, and journalist and world-wide traveller Dave Minton.

The purple *'Sport* was produced by Tee Publications, to complement its ever-popular *Motor Sport* magazine, which had started as the *Brooklands Gazette* in 1925. *Motorcycle Sport* was founded and edited by Cyril Quantrill, who started it in April 1962 as a newspaper to rival *Motorcycle News*, of which he had also been the founding editor in 1955. Cyril Ayton, who had cut his journalist teeth on the Green 'Un, *Motor Cycling*, took over *MCS* from Cyril Quantrill, and, under his editorship, it became a magazine in November 1962. The majority of articles in *'Sport* were written by freelance writers, most of them biking enthusiasts rather than journalists. The magazine had a select but dedicated readership. Its small circulation made it difficult to get a lot of advertising, but it was a fascinating job. The total staff of *'Sport* was Cyril and I.

One year, I rode the Press Trial on the trials MAC, it was hard on the old bike, with one section that went down into a gulley and out the other side, I fell off going down the slope, gathered myself and machine together, but failed to climb out the other side, looped it, ending up down the bottom for the second time: I won the trophy for the best crash of the day!

I roamed far and wide to get advertising revenue. One day I was in North Leicester Motorcycles in Coalville, Leicestershire, talking to owner Stuart when his phone rang. After he put it down he said that it was some fella in the Isle of Man who sent him his Ducati heads for shimming the tappets, but it was a valve-spring model. I was in a position to tell him this was from my £1000 Manx Grand Prix mount from 1980!

In later years Cyril was never keen on the foreign jollies, so not long after I joined *MCS* he set me up for a weekend in Italy to see the new range of Pirelli tyres. We flew down, attended a press presentation, and had a fine meal that night. They had provided all the journos with a free helmet. Next day, when they finally gathered up the die-hard alkies (no names, but one was found asleep in the dining room!), we were bussed out of town, some off-roaders were dropped at a fearsome looking scrambles track, whist the rest of us were taken to Pirelli's road test facility. Parked there was a selection of Laverda and Guzzi machinery. We left the paddock, but had to return through there, so no one was doing 'fast laps.' A couple of the journos were not riders, but they felt safe enough to accompany me on various laps on a Guzzi Californian. In the nearby woods were half a dozen Fantics, plus a few sections to try. There were a couple of 45-gallon drums on their sides, I reckoned I could ride over them; trouble was, as soon as I touched one, they rolled forward with me! I managed to extract myself without needing hospital assistance. Another track was the wet ride, with the ability to drench the surface. I was the first to find it, there was a timing board to measure the time each lap took. I was enjoying this when the Pirelli man came and asked if I wanted it watering – "No thanks" I said. He was most impressed that I managed to deck the Laverda crankcase, something Pete Davies always did when he raced the Jota for Roger Slater. Others came over, but I think my time was not beaten by many. I caught up with Julian Ryder at one point, I changed up as he changed down, that was nearly a calamity!

A wonderful two day's play away, a new helmet, and at no cost. Want a job as a motorcycling journo? I met Terry Snelling, an *MCN* staff man on that trip, I have no family connection, but after a few drinks I tried to convince him I was a long lost brother!

I had been using Nikwax leather cleaner and proofer for a while, and wondered if the company would like to advertise its products in *'Sport*, so I popped down to their Sussex factory. They had never given a thought to promoting their products to motorcyclists, but I believe it makes a good contribution to their coffers now.

Another time I was on a visit to Mortimer Engineering (MEL), in Rochester; they produced fairings and rearsets for the Japanese machines before they themselves produced sports models. I knew they were importing a new machine to kit out with their goodies, it took a while to find out it was the Honda VT250, which Honda produced in a valiant attempt to pinch sales from the LC Yamaha. A colleague of Mortimer Engineering went into a Japanese Honda dealer and bought one of the first consignments, still in its crate, and freighted it straight to the UK. The next week I was back on the Isle of Man, and noticed the registration letter 'V' was being introduced. I managed to get V250 MAN held for me. As the VT250 had come into the UK without a (V50) form, I had to present the machine to the Manx licensing authority for them to check engine and frame numbers, so, borrowing a pair of trade plates, I rode the machine to Liverpool and across. A super handling machine, but it was never going to outgun the sports strokers that were flooding the market.

As it was a model destined for the Japanese home market, there was a red dash light that lit up when you got to 50km/h. I did not mention it to the odd person I let ride it, they came back, thinking they had broken it! The machine is now in the hands of a Honda enthusiast, and still retains its V250 MAN registration. 'Sport managed to scoop MCN on that one.

I was at a Honda Press Day at Donington. A Saltbox friend, Chris Bryant, was working for the PR side of the Japanese giant. We discussed the VT250, and I quietly said "I have one." He didn't bite at that, but later in the day, I pulled the Manx logbook out of my pocket and showed it to him, he was astonished, to say the least! We had the idea to take it to Power Road, Chiswick and photograph it as if we had just stolen it, but bottled out of this idea!

FROM TWO TO THREE AND FOUR WHEELS

I returned to live on the Island in the late '70s, though continued to go back and forth for several years. In 1982 I took a Reliant Robin back to the Island with me. It was cheap, and you could drive it on a bike licence. When I bought it the whole interior was covered in a blue mock fur, it was like a blue furry cave! I spent the whole journey back, ripping lumps of this off and hurling it out of the window! The Reliant Robin is notoriously unstable; once, going a bit hasty past the Liverpool Arms between Laxey and Douglas, my foot slipped off the gas, and the thing rose onto two wheels, with the body scraping on the road; I had visions of everything above the screen being wiped off, so laid my head on the passenger seat, when it resumed forward motion on three wheels, and me peering out from the passenger's side; Mr Bean couldn't have done it any funnier!

I drove it for many months, then decided to get a car licence. A shooting mate, Harry Dale was a driving instructor; it wasn't so much that he had to teach me to drive, it was to rid me of the undesirable habits I had picked up over many years, like crossing your arms! I managed to get through the test first time. Leaving the test centre Harry said, "Well you can go back to your bad habits now."

TRIPS ABROAD WITH MATES

A group of us Velo and Speedway fans made the trip over to Assen in Holland in 1981 to watch the ice speedway world final: four fairly bulky figures in a Mini Metro. We took in the Dutch TT race track, as it was then, mainly roads, but barred to two-wheeled traffic. They should have barred Metros: at one point there were four wheels and three passengers squealing in sympathy! The ice race final is held over two days, a Saturday evening, and the afternoon on Sunday. It has a terrific atmosphere, it is much better 'live' at the event than on TV, and well worth making a trip over to see the ice gladiators.

Our second trip was to the Eindhoven final, the following year. We had probably drunk our duty-free by the first night: it was Jenever Old Gin from the earthenware bottle – mm! On this trip, we took some mates from the Croydon Shooting Club who fancied a weekend away. We did not tell them what to expect when the tapes went up for the first race, and the four riders came through on their elbows! Eindhoven is the centre for the Philips electrical brand, so we stopped in at the Evoluon, which was at the time a saucer-shaped state-of-the-art museum, but is now a conference centre. We also took in Bruges, a lovely canal-side town on our way home.

One day in 1982, I was passing Bruce and Brenda Preston's house in New Malden, near London, so dropped in to say hello. Bruce was the Director of the British Motorcyclist Foundation. The place was in chaos: Bruce and Brenda, their family and friends were in the process of moving Clarrie Williams, a BMW-owning friend to Ybbs in Austria, but had only a limited amount of space in which to stow his possessions, and the group of people accompanying them. "Why not take the Metro?" I suggested, adding "but you'll have to take me as well!" "Be back here in under an hour with your passport," was the retort. I rang Mum to find it, shot home, gathered a few things and legged it back to New Malden. "Where we going?" "Follow that van!" And off we set. Through France, into Austria, a two-day 700-mile dash. I can't recall much of the journey, I was glued to the tail of the VW transporter as we made our way to Ybbs on the Danube, a beautiful area of Austria. We arrived just before New Year's Eve – Silvester, as it is known there – so preparations were in full swing. Not wishing to spend the whole evening drinking, myself and Martin Roberts took ourselves off to visit Melk, the site of the forthcoming FIM International Touring Rally. We carried on finding small roads, some with white and red poles either side, but there was little snow to be seen that year. One road we took went higher and higher, and narrower and narrower; then we saw the Austrian flags on the telegraph poles, I was convinced the next one would show the Czech flag! We decided to turn round. The road was narrow, on one side was a bank, and on the other side all we could see were the tips of giant fir trees! A multipoint turn was required, and we high-tailed it back into civilisation, and Ybbs, to rejoin the celebration we had left many hours ago. A trip to be remembered.

I arrived home on Thursday, weary after that trip, and the next day was the MCC Exeter Trial. I hadn't entered that year, but Geoff Blanthorn fancied a sight of the event, so I climbed wearily back into the Metro and headed west. We didn't fancy driving straight home, so stopped the night at the Half Moon coaching house, in Sherborne, Dorset. On the menu was an 'Ilchester steak' cooked in Guinness – delicious! I survived just one drink before heading off to my pit, whereupon the bottom two legs of the bed collapsed, I was so tired, I slept that night at about a 45-degree angle!

THE ARBUTHNOT TRIAL

From 1919 through to 1939, there was a trial for Royal Navy personnel, The Arbuthnot Trial, in memory of Sir Robert Arbuthnot. He rode the TT and finished third in the Single Cylinder class in 1908. He was lost at the battle of Jutland, and his third-place Triumph went down with his ship, HMS Defence.

In the 1980s Ian Rennie found an old route card and decided to reinstate the event; I rode the first one in 1982 on the Triumph 3HW, it was a glorious blast along the South Downs, where I had never ridden before.

DESPATCH RIDING

Being ad man for '*Sport* was not a lucrative occupation, so in 1984 I left and joined a growing band of despatch riders based in London. You certainly earned a good wage, but you also spent a fair deal on fuel, spares and renewing clothing, you could wear out an oversuit in a year. By this time I had come back to the mainland for a spell in 1981 when Dad became ill. I lost him in 1982, and then Mum in 1988.

Some particular jobs from this time stand out; I remember having to be at Weston-super-Mare for a collection at 9am (early start) to be delivered back to South London, then a pick up in North London to be delivered to Manchester Airport: 750 miles in a day!

One of the jobs with a visual bonus was to collect the day's takings from a lunch club called 'Naughty Lunches' and lodge it in their bank in Regent Street; they can't have spent much on wages, as the young ladies there were very scantily dressed! I had been passed a Police Everoak helmet, which I disguised with a red tape decoration. One day, the pickled clientele in the club were getting a little out of hand, I walked in, still helmet clad. Under red lights, the stripes disappeared and I looked like The Old Bill. The uproar subsided and the woman in charge asked me to hang around until they got things sorted out. As well as an eyeful of pretty young maidens, I got a £20 tip that day!

I had a parcel to deliver in Tottenham; when I arrived the area was thick with police, personnel and vans, something was going on. As I turned into the estate I spotted the name – Broadwater Farm – it was November, 1985 and PC Keith Blakelock had only recently been murdered there. I retraced my steps back to the office, with the package marked 'Undeliverable,' and the controller said "You weren't the first to abort a delivery there." Other times, when delivering packages from abroad, we would be escorted into an empty room, and were left there to open the package, with cameras trained on your every move. We could have been carrying a bomb, or illicit goods.

Another job was to collect from a horticultural shop in Twickenham for delivery in Bromley. The address for collection was closed, but a chap was sitting in a car outside. I was given a seed packet, with instructions to take it directly to Bromley. I didn't know what was in the packet, but a few of the other despatch guys guessed that it contained narcotics. I arrived in Bromley, I didn't have to look for the address, there was a chap waiting on the pavement for me!

I know Dave Richmond, who wrote the road riding column for *Motor Cycling Weekly*, and he persuaded me to write a despatch riders' column for them. There was the odd perk, Kawasaki decked out a Scorpion 350 with fairing and top box, for me to ride and evaluate. The belt rear drive used to make it hard to wheel out

(continues page 49)

Camping days at Weymouth. Dad and yours truly with his first Vincent, HHR 451.

A full load! Yours truly at the helm, big sis Tricia at the rear, and family friends between, Weymouth.

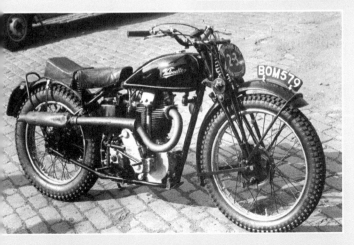

Billy Tiffen's 1936 Scottish Six Days Trial-winning Velocette KSS.

Junior Wing Nut! An exceedingly brushed up yours truly in a school picture, about the only time I wore a tie!

Dad at his day job. A dental technician by trade through the war years and into the '70s, he was my odd-job boy and driver to race meetings.

Awheel! In the back garden at Santon Villas during TT 1960, gingerly taking my first powered ride on the Houghton Blaby, shepherded by Charlie Murray, owner of the Murray's Museum.
Right: Posing with the Houghton Blaby outside Santon Villas, TT 1960.

Dad's first Vincent, HHR 451, after being rescued from a shed where it had lain for over 30 years – scrubbed up well, didn't it. It has now been re-sold to a Vincent enthusiast in Belgium.

Mum and Dad with grandchild Rebecca at my sister's smallholding in Chawston, Bedfordshire, with their second Vincent, RGW 798.

E B Christian's North Quay depot, my first workplace on the Island. The garage housed the turntable.

Mansfield Corner at a very wet Cadwell Park! The 100-miler meeting, 1972. I scored my only race victory at that meeting, beating all the 500s on my Viper.

Mike Hailwood (Ducati) riding back to the pits after remounting following a fall at Glen Helen, 1960 Ultra Lightweight TT.

Stan Lewis ploughs on up-river on his Mk 1 KSS, 'the little rough-un.' Picture taken on Sunrising Hill on the Banbury Run.

Ollie 'somebody' on the Viceroy I later bought from him. Time has erased his name from my failing memory bank!

Mum and Dad at a Cadwell Park High Speed Trial meeting.

Arthur and Brenda Lavington, with his mechanic Roy Church, at the TT weigh-in.

Mum and myself pose on the Series D Vincent, complete with trailer.

Chatting all things Veloce. Reg ?? (forgotten surname), Bertie Goodman (Veloce Ltd) and a partly-obscured Arthur Lavington at a Federation of National One Make Clubs (thankfully later called the BMF) Rally. The Model O and Roarer were being displayed. Holding the van up is Roger Jennings, a former racer who is currently still involved in Velo machines.

A 1930s production line at Hall Green. It looked much the same in the 1960s!

Pegging the tent steady at the first Dragon Rally, Bryan Bras, 1962.

Mick Miller and mechanic unload his 7R at Jurby Airfield, 1962.

'Noddy' John Wheeler (Velocette) in the 1962 Senior Manx Grand Prix.

Joe Dunphy (Beart Norton) 1962 Senior Manx Grand Prix. I was a member of his signalling team at the Gooseneck that year.

My first trial. I got less bad as the years progressed!

VINTAGE MOTOR CYCLE CLUB
(Southern Region)

RESULTS

REG. ASCOTT TROPHY TRIAL
DEWS FARM PITS 10 March 1963

Reg. Ascott Trophy:	D. DESBOROUGH.	247cc. 1930 Levis.	3 Marks Lost.
Best up to 250cc:	A. R. CLEAR.	1929 Ariel.	31 " "
Best 251 to 350cc:	R. D. THOMAS.	1926 Douglas.	18 " "
Best over 350cc:	R. GLADING.	490cc. 1928 Norton.	17 " "
Next 10% of entries:	E. WATSON.	1930 Velocette.	23 " "
	B. N. CLARKE.	490cc. 1927 Norton.	24 " "
Best Performance on Standard Road Tyres:	K. DENMAN.	1925 Raleigh.	29 " "
Novice Award:	J. F. PARTRIDGE.	1930 Velocette.	33 " "

Q.	Name	Machine	1.	2.	3.	4.	5.	6.	7.	8.	9.	10.	Total
							MARKS LOST						
Machines up to 250cc.													
5.	W. Snelling. (N)	1930 Ariel (SRT)	5.	5.	3.	5.	5.	1.	3.	3.	3.	5.	38.
6.	R. Forrest. (N)	1926 B.S.A.	3.	3.	3.	5.	5.	0.	5.	3.	5.	3.	35.
7.	J. Mitchell. (N)	1926 B.S.A.	5.	5.	3.	5.	5.	3.	3.	5.	5.	5.	44.
8.	E.L.Wade.	1930 Ariel.	5.	3.	3.	5.	5.	1.	3.	3.	5.	3.	34.
0.	D.Desborough.	1930 Levis.	0.	3.	0.	0.	0.	0.	0.	0.	0.	0.	3.
1.	C.Desborough.				N O N		S T A R T E R						
2.	A. R. Clear. (N)	1929 Ariel (SRT)	5.	5.	3.	5.	3.	1.	0.	3.	3.	3.	31.
Machines 251cc to 350cc.													
3.	J.P.Griffith.	1930 Velo.			N O N		S T A R T E R						
4.	K. Denman.	1925 Raleigh (SRT).	3.	3.	3.	3.	0.	5.	3.	3.	3.		29.
5.	R. D. Thomas.	1926 Douglas.	5.	3.	3.	0.	3.	0.	5.	3.	0.	1.	18.
6.	E. A. Hewett.	1926 A.J.S. (SRT)	5.	3.	3.	3.	3.	3.	3.	5.	3.	3.	34.
7.	J.W.W.Gough.	1928 Sunbeam.	3.	3.	3.	3.	0.	5.	3.	3.	5.	3.	31.
8.	E. E. Thompson.	1930 Velo.	3.	3.	5.	5.	0.	5.	5.	0.	3.		32.
0.	C.J.Grout.	1930 Velo.	3.	3.	5.	0.	0.	3.	3.	5.	3.		26.
0.	E.Watson.	1930 Velo.	5.	3.	5.	5.	1.	0.	1.	0.	0.		23.
9.	J. F. Partridge (N)	1930 Velo.	3.	3.	3.	5.	3.	5.	3.	0.	3.		33.
Machines over 350cc.													
9.	T. M. Cook.	1928 Ariel.	5.	5.	3.	3.	5.	0.	1.	0.	0.	3.	25.
1.	F. P. Heath.	1926 A.J.S.			N O N		S T A R T E R						
2.	K. Blake.	1915 Triumph.			N O N		S T A R T E R						
3.	R. Glading.	1928 Norton.	0.	0.	3.	5.	0.	3.	0.	0.			17.
4.	B. N. Clarke.	1927 Norton (SRT)	5.	3.	3.	1.	3.	0.	0.	1.	3.	5.	24.
5.	L. Lord (N)	1927 Norton.	5.	5.	5.	3.	5.	0.	0.	5.	0.	5.	33.

Somewhere in Kent, trying out Jeff Clew's Model U trials Velo (known as 'Eustace') at a Vintage trial.

Jeff and Audrey Clew, Velo fans through and through, with one of Jeff's many two-stroke Velos.

Terry Moore awaits to start the Manx Scooter Rally. The starter is J Graham Oates, whose motorcycle exploits (trans-Canada, first person to reach Hudson Bay on a rubber-tyred vehicle, TT rider etc) I chronicled in *Aurora to Ariel; The Motorcycling Life of J Graham Oates, a Pioneering Manx Motorcyclist.*

Arthur Lavington (Velocette KSS), in the 1949 Junior Clubman TT, before the fork spring broke at Hillberry and threw him down the road!

Arthur Lavington at Signpost Corner, 1958 Junior TT. This was before he fitted Velo teles.

Velocette's untested prewar supercharged twin, the Roarer, outside Arthur Lavington's workshop in Tooting.

Arthur Lavington at Quarter Bridge on the Thruxton in the 1967 Production TT.

Geoff Dodkin scrutineers Keith Heckles' Production Commando, 1971 Production TT.

The Veloce catalogue picture of a Thruxton, showing the rear mudguard stay that was never used.

Assembling the last batch of Indian Velos at the rear of Geoff Dodkin's shop.

An Indian Velocette, made by American Floyd Clymer using an Italian chassis and wheels. Geoff Dodkin bought the remaining stock when the company was folded up.

The Saltbox club badge. I am still in contact with members of the Biggin Hill Club some 50 years after I left the area.

Joint Presidents of the Saltbox MCC, Swiss Champion Fritz Scheidegger and his English passenger John Robinson.

Paul Coombs (CRD) waits to start a practice lap, 1968 Manx Grand Prix.

The Saltbox Club prepares to parade along Douglas Prom at the 60th anniversary TT meeting. Del Whitton, on his MCC A7 BSA, heads the crew.

In the back yard of the Christian's house, Woodbourne Road, Douglas. I am checking the rear chain, with Del Whitton, Brian Sprawson and Pete Jenner hatching some devilish plan to inflict on the family!

The Saltbox clan, at my TT photo exhibition.

Caught me a big'un! Fishing off the Port St Mary Breakwater, I brought in this long portion of cat food!

Barry Sheene pushes back to the pits after falling off and wiping the electrics off the Kawasaki 3.

EVENT 8 : 6 LAP RACE FOR SOLOS TO 500 c.c. (Fastest lap No 113 in 1m.35.8s., 56.37 mph)

Place	No.	Name	Machine	Laps	Time M. S.	Speed M.P.H.	Remarks
1	115	W Snelling	1962 Velocette	6	9 58.8	54.11	1st Award
2	113	Malcolm Elgar	1969 Egli-Vincent	6	9 59.2	54.07	2nd Award
3	106	Phil Williams	1965 Vel. Thruxton	6	10 19.2	52.33	
4	116	Ian Fray	1965 Vel. Venom	6	10 19.4	52.31	
5	111	Stuart Dobson	1968 Velocette	6	10 22.6	52.04	
6	112	Derrick Bishop	1958 Ariel	6	10 24.2	51.91	
7	118	Paul Croft	1959 Velocette	6	10 26.0	51.76	
8	42	Frank Chapman	1954 Ariel VHA	6	10 28.4	51.56	
9	49	Bob Gesson	1968 Suzuki	6	11 04.0	48.8	
10	104	Melvin Cooper	1969 Vel. Thruxton	6	11 18.4	47.76	
11	117	Peter Miles	1969 Vel. Venom	6	11 23.8	47.38	1st Novice Aw.
12	1	Peter Biles	1951 Vincent Comet	6	11 33.8	46.7	1st StV Award
13	101	Hilary Musson	1968 Triumph T100T	6	11 38.0	46.42	

My only race win! By .04 of a second at the 1972 Cadwell Park Vincent Owners HST meeting ...

... and this is the Malcolm Elgar Egli Comet that I raced against (and beat) at the Vincent Owners HST meeting at Cadwell Park, 1972. This picture was taken at the 1000 Bikes Rally at Mallory Park.

The Ferndale riders, with their haul of booty, from TT 1972. Left to right, Hugh Evans, Ray Knight, Roger Bowler, Alan Walsh and Ron Baylie.

Alan Walsh (Triumph), prior to his whoopsie in the pits, 1972 Production TT.

My first Island house! The Green Tent, Tromode Road, with a colour coordinated Green MAC.

Charlie and 'Em Murray leave the Grandstand on their Triumph outfit in a '60s Vintage Club Manx Rally.

The Press Trial; I had already fallen off the MAC entering the section, I was just about to loop it on the way out, that's why I won best crash of the day!

They should have pegged the drums down! Playing with a Fantic at a Pirelli test day, Italy.

Cyril Ayton prepares to head off on the VT250.

A helmeted Cyril Ayton prepares to test ride the Honda VT250. Tom Mortimer and 'short-portly' in attendance.

Honda test day at Donington Park. Trying to keep up with Ray Knight on a VF400!

Too much Genever (old gin!) with Geoff Blanthorn in Holland for the ice racing.

Captain Sir Robert Keith Arbuthnot, 4th Baronet at the 1908 TT.

of the garage first thing in the morning, but as it got heat in it was a lot easier. I learnt the meaning of 'freelance' whist writing this column, I wrote for free as I got 'lanced' by *MCW*! Dave was my mentor in journalism, he taught me the ground rules, how to encompass all in a story, not to keep the subject too rigid, perhaps to waffle a bit, which is maybe what you are reading now! Dave now lives on a smaller Island to the south of the UK called Wight, we regularly correspond through the electric medium of Facebook. He has constructed a wonderful website: https://motorcycletimeline.com/ with features and stories from the very birth of motorcycling – you can easily lose yourself for hours browsing the pages, as he paints a vivid picture of riding 80 years ago.

Sidewinder, which made the flexible sidecar to get round the 250 limit law, had bought out a trailer, suitable for use with a solo; the Europeans had been trailering for many years. The company persuaded Yamaha to connect it to a 600, and I was let loose. It was impractical for London streets, the number of times it got bashed as someone moved out, not expecting me to be trailering. It was also a bugger to back up, so I did not use it for long for work in and around London. To test the stability of the thing, I filled it with sacks of spuds and hammered up and down the Caterham Bypass one evening, accelerating and braking; it was a very stable unit. I believe out-of-town despatchers did buy it.

During the course of this job I encountered a lot of women (of all ages) opening the door in their dressing gown (does a dressing gown have a door?) – or sometimes less. One geezer answered the door holding a towel in front of him; behind him (big behind) was a mirror!

It was not unknown for customers not to have goods or services ready on time. To save face for them, we had to say we had a puncture or a cable breakage which resulted in late delivery; we often copped a few extra bob for taking the stick on delivery. I reckon some weeks I did a thousands miles a week, mostly in and around London. It was a young man's game, and I wouldn't fancy doing it in London nowadays.

After leaving Concorde Couriers I despatched on my Guzzi V50. One day, coming back on the Kingston Bypass, it dropped onto one cylinder; I cursed Italian electrics and rode home on a 250. We could not trace the problem, so stripped the engine. The left hand barrel came off, complete with the conrod! The big end cap had broken, the piston had come up, got stuck in the carbon and the rod was just laying in the bore, not damaging anything. A new rod, gaskets and seals sorted it out, and it was back on the road again.

In the meantime, to keep earning, I had borrowed Dad's Mini Metro (this was in 1985, so I had my driving licence by then). I decided that this was the way to go, so got a Citroën C15 van, which was the most-used tool for despatchers at that time. There was a company in London that was selling them at a big discount, because it was selling dozens a week. I rang my mate at Eurocars, the Citroën dealer on the Isle of Man, and put it to him that I would buy from him, if he matched their price. After much spluttering on the phone he said "Yes, but don't ever tell anyone the deal we did." I flew back to the Island on a Friday, collected the van and did a few hundred miles over the weekend. Monday morning I took it in for its first service, then got on the boat back. Ringing up the courier company, I managed to get a job bringing goods from Manchester back to London.

Another time I took pallet of paper, which I had collected at 4am in Wandsworth, south London, to be delivered in Hull, by 9am. As usual, when you had dropped off goods, you rang the office to confirm delivery. A job had just come in from Ikea, which was based in Hull. The company had been sent a load of units without handles from Sweden. I collected the goods, but instead of taking them to the airport, I was instructed to bring them down to their London depot. That saved them a lot of time, and that part of the job paid for the fuel there and back.

I did 52,000 miles in the Citroën van in a year. Because I was (technically) living on the Isle of Man during this time, my van bore Manx number plates. I was pulled over once in Tooting by a police officer and an excise officer, who didn't recognise the Manx tax disc. It was perfectly legal. The next week, the same excise officer tried to pull me over again, took one look and waved me on!

One company I worked for was based just round the corner from the Tooting Police Station at Amen Corner. A female constable accused me of taking the whiz with a 'foreign' registered vehicle in London. I asked her if she saw me at weekends, because I run goods to and from the Island at the weekend and deliver during the week. As if I would take the whiz!

Living on the Island

AMULREE AND LOSSAN Y TWOAIE

My first proper abode in the Island was a very small semi-detached house on the Glen Road, Laxey. It was called Bluebell Cottage, which I thought a bit twee. Looking through the deeds I found it had for years been named Amulree, which is a borough in the parish of Perth and Kinross in Scotland. Amulree was also a hill used on the London to Edinburgh MCC trial, it proved to be a stopper for most of the entry in 1922. The Edinburgh Trial is now run in Derbyshire, and was the only one of the three classic trials that I won the motorcycle class outright, so I felt it appropriate to change the name of the house back to Amulree, and call my publishing efforts Amulree Publications.

Before buying it, I was walking round the outside of what I thought was the whole house, when a head popped out. Rene McKevitt informed me that what I was hoping to buy was in fact only half of what I thought was one house. She invited me in for a cup of tea, and she wished me luck in getting the house, it cost me £4750 in 1978. Rene was a lovely neighbour, she would occasionally pop in when I was at work, take down, clean and re-hang the net curtains. Whilst I was off-Island seeing to my parents, Rene would open doors and windows to air the place. In July, 2016, Rene celebrated her 100th birthday, still living at Amulree No 2 (my place was Amulree No 1), but she sadly passed away in her 101st year.

Amulree was too small to accommodate Pat, her Rottweiler Briw and myself, so in 2012 we looked around and bought an old (1928) wooden bungalow just further up the Glen Road. It was then called Heidebloem (Dutch for Heather) when we bought it, but Pat renamed it Lossan y Twoaie, which is Manx for 'Northern Lights,' a fitting name considering my association with J Graham Oates and the Aurora motorcycle, and with Pat living in Canada for a period and seeing them over there. Trouble is, every time I go to purchase something over the phone, I end up having to spell the name out. Luckily we have some good post people, because some parcels come with very strange addresses. I also get letters addressed to Swelling, Smelling, Snowing – I don't care as long as the cheques don't bounce! We have seen the Northern Lights at frequent intervals here on the Island, looking spectacular.

The house has Manx motorcycle connections, too. During WW II, the Craine family lived there whilst the husband was at sea in the merchant navy. The son of the family was Dennis Craine, who went on to win the 1965 Lightweight Manx on a Greeves. Perhaps a blue plaque might be appropriate?

In the early '70s, the house was rented during the TT by the Kelly family, not a Manx Kelly though. Peter Kelly, formerly the editor of *Old Bike Mart*, rented the place for the whole family to stay during the TT. He was so taken with it, he took a series of photographs home and got a local artist to paint a picture with all the family members and their bikes in. It was suggested that it would make a suitable picture for a jigsaw, so it was added to the Gibson catalogue.

In 2019, a combination of high rainfall, high tide and somewhat inept river management (leaving a hole in the river wall), meant that the Laxey river and the Glen Road shared the same water level. The first we knew was when Lyndon Powell waded across the river/road to see if we were okay. The water came up and over the verandah, but stopped at the front door. Our old 1928 wooden bungalow is built on a concrete plinth, the water flowed under and around us. We lost a back room and a car port, but were able to continue living there. 17 other properties up and down the road were not so fortunate, some being flooded by two feet of water! Ten months on, some of these houses are still not habitable. Our car got picked up by the current, floated down stream/road and crushed against a stone wall. We got very lucky that day!

ANDREAS RACING ASSOCIATION

During the 1970s, the Andreas Racing Association's home tracks were at Jurby Airfield and the Jurby South Road Course, and I rode there from 1974 to 1980 on machines ranging from Velos to Saab-engined Norton and Ducati. The club name should really have been the Jurby Racing Association. They had agreements in place to race at Andreas, the other former RAF airfield in the North of the Island, but at the last minute, that agreement fell through so they took on Jurby. The initial course ran past the hangars, some of which held a concrete manufacturing plant. It depended how many blocks they made, as to how close the course went to the hangar. It was rough, bumpy and loose, many took to shrouding the front of their forks and helmet with tape, to save the shot-blast effect.

I well remember one race, I was scrapping with John Dickenson (Yamaha) and Allan Hannay (Suzuki GS1000). Suddenly, I got a face-full of oil, something was amiss somewhere. At the end of the main runway straight, the Suzuki went down; he had worn through the engine casing. I headed John, but went down myself on the last left-hander of the hangar section, the oily front end sliding away. I retrieved the bike and carried on, and a couple of corners later, there was John on the floor. That day, Graham Cannell outlasted us all to win the 500 class, his first race win.

Other times I had plenty of scraps with Neil Kelly. At that time, Neil was riding a 400+ Honda in the four-stroke class. He was the last TT winner on a

Velocette, the 1967 500 Production, so it was satisfying to put it over him; not that often, but we did head him home a couple of times.

The Jurby South Road circuit was a triangle of roads, very fast; my Velo was timed at 120+ on the Ballavarran Straight. Ray Knight rode his last race there when his 600 Harris Honda went down big time on the coast road and pretty well knocked all the corners off. We were able to take the remnants back to John Harris Motorcycles in Kent in a Peugeot 106 van. The doctor went to see Ray in hospital, with his NHS files and his racing licence: let's say there was a slight date discrepancy! The doctor retired Ray from racing that day, but he later helped start the ARA race school.

BERNIE LUND

I briefly worked for Bernie Lund at Grand Prix Motorcycles, Ramsey in 1981. Bernie sold mainly Suzuki and CZ machines. He had been in business for about a year when I arrived. Let's just say Bernie was not too hot on paperwork. Every invoice from day one was piled up on a table, I had to turn the pile over, and set to and construct a set of accounts from that paper tower, I had to quiz bike buyers how much he had given them in part-exchange for machines, it was a nightmare. I sorted things out, made a year's accounts and VAT return, but left him to sign it, so if anything was wrong, he was going to get the blame! I also remember a few interesting customers during my time there.

Sam Clutton had bought a 125 CZ from Bernie. Sam was an acknowledged musical organ expert, they used to fly him across to Westminster Abbey to keep their organ in top nick. He came in to say that the bike should do 59mph, but he could only achieve 50, so could we sort it? Well, I set to, and quickly discovered that the fixed point spigot was loose. I repaired this, but how could a 'short portly' achieve the required speed. I rode it up to the Gooseneck and back, it seemed okay, so we called Sam back to collect it. Gratifyingly, he reported back that all was well, it now achieved 59mph – phew! Sam also owned an 1908 GP Itala, a 12,000cc four-cylinder monster of a car (3000cc per cylinder!). I recall seeing him harry an E-type across the railway lines past the Bungalow in it one day, this in a car with no front brakes.

A lady called Pat McQuaid had bought a Demm Dove from Bernie, but it was not running too well. She lived near Ramsey Hairpin, and was responsible for designing one of the Manx tartans, the one sold at Tynwald Mill, as opposed to the one from the Laxey Woollen Mill. She was quite a modest, timorous person and did not ride the machine hard enough to keep the exhaust clear of soot. My job was to blast it up and over the Mountain. After about five miles of this, there was almost a fire coming from the exhaust pipe as all the oil was burnt out. Then it was good for a few more months, after which we repeated the process.

One day, when the International Six Days Trial was on, we had to do some subtle repairs to a Met Police competitor's Triumph at the back of the shop – he had pranged it above Ramsey – but we got it back on the road again.

Bernie's son Alan, a successful trials and scramble rider, now runs Road and Track Motorcycles in Tynwald Street, Douglas.

I left Bernie's in 1982, when I moved back to the mainland because my father was ailing. He passed away in 1982, and I then stayed on until Mum passed in 1988. The solicitors sat on Dad's probate for over a year; in that time house prices crashed and we lost about a third of the value. They waived their fees because of their inefficiency, not that that helped a lot! Having been away for a long time, I went back to resume life on the Island for good in 1988.

When I returned, I enrolled in a couple of Manx History and Archaeology evening classes, and the whole Island came alive for me. There is so much to see and do here, I am still finding new places to this day. The two tutors I had could not be more different; Sheila Cregeen (who made fantastic fudge) was like a wire-haired terrier, and Larch Garrad, one of the Manx Museum's assistant keepers, was a cat lover, and looked like a big tabby. One day, after a heavy storm, we were beach-combing on the shore at the foot of the Ballaugh cliffs, when I stumbled across a big piece of Mull Hill pottery dating back to 3500BC, that had dropped from the receding cliffs. I took it to the Museum the next day, they hadn't got a piece that big.

Mates

IAN KERR MBE

I got to know Ian Kerr when he was writing articles for *Motorcycle Sport*, and used to drop by Standard House: being a serving police officer, he used to leave his patrol car on the yellow lines! For some years, Ian was my riding companion on the MCC trials. When Ian came to the TT, he either hijacked one of our cars, or whatever two-wheeler I had at the time (I wouldn't be using it, being at the photo exhibition all day). One year, he borrowed our Peugeot 106 van; he was supposed to leave it in the airport car park after the Senior TT and jet home. Later that day, we went searching for it, but where had the bugger hidden it? After exhaustive sweeps of the car park, we came home to an apologetic phone call. Within about half a mile of the pits, the cambelt had broken, and lifted the camshaft clean out of the head! He got a lift down to Ronaldsway so didn't miss his plane. That was a write-off. Another time, we had a rusty Ford Fiesta, which ran on gas. He was bimbling around when it suddenly spun on him; he was sitting there facing the rear subframe and wheels! I told him it was a rust bucket! It was last seen being driven round a scrapyard on two front wheels.

Sometimes, he struck it lucky. He bought a Vauxhall that was going to be scrapped for £20, with a full tank of fuel. At the end of the week, someone offered him £250 for it, I guess he didn't refuse!

He didn't goose everything we lent him. My recent two-wheel transport was a 400 Suzuki Burgman: with my hips it is not easy getting on a bike. Ian was scooting around on it one wet day, being somewhat hassled by big bikes. After a few miles of this, he got hacked off and gave that Burgman some real dixie (it does over 90), dropping all those tyros. You didn't get an MBE for services to motorcycle safety without being a first-class rider on all machines (but I still beat him in some MCC trials).

Mum nearly had a fit one day when a police Range Rover pulled up outside the house, lights flashing; it was just Ian paying a social call!

MIKE VANGUCCI

Mike is an amazing rider and engineer, who excelled in all forms of our sport. He decided to build a trials MAC, and I had enough bits strewn around our garage in Mitcham to make one, so he popped down one Saturday. He left with plenty enough bits to build the bike, and more besides. The next weekend, he rang up for tappet clearances! He had stripped everything down to their constituent parts, made one good engine out of three, rebuilt the gearbox and was ready to sally forth!

When the European Union deal was ratified in 1972, members of the Vintage Club rode to Brussels. Mike rode a single-speed Ariel, which entailed stopping and restarting at every traffic light, junction etc.

KEN LAW
Ken was another Dorking Velo club TT stopover on our little island. His mounts were a MK II KSS with a McKenzie or McCandless swinging arm conversion, and an LE. He also built the Mongrel, with the Valiant frame, but LE engine and radiator. They were basically the same power unit, but the Valiant was air-cooled, and the Noddy was water cooled. They pepped the LE engine a bit when they made the Valiant, but it was still using the fragile LE bottom end. Veloce provided dealers with decompression spacers for under the barrels to detune the bike slightly and give the bearings an easier life. These were fitted when they came in for service; it must have been strange to have a bike feeling more sluggish after a service.

HUGH AND EUNICE EVANS
At the 1967 TT Hugh Evans and Giacomo Agostini had at least one thing in common; they were both listed as riding MVs in the Senior TT – but on very different machines: Ago was on the four-cylinder Fire Engine, Hugh's was a 175 MV chassis housing a BSA A50 engine. One more difference; Hugh finished, Ago went out with a broken chain after a titanic battle with Mike Hailwood (MV vs Honda)

Hugh ran Aitchee Engineering at Biggin Hill aerodrome, and I worked for him for a while. One day, before the Biggin Hill air display, we were buzzed by a Vulcan that was practicing for the forthcoming show; it was like a football field flying just a few feet over our heads!

Eunice also raced, she started her career on a BSA Bantam, and finished on a 500 Honda Four. In between she raced and won the Ladies race at Cadwell Park on Hugh's BSA, beating Andrea Herron, TT-winner Tom Herron's wife.

One of Hugh's friends, who flew the Decca plane, wanted to check the radio on his own private plane, and invited me to go aloft with him. He gave me the tiller and said, "keep it straight and level," while he got his head down checking the radio. All was well, until it suddenly ascended at quite a rate of knots; we had flown over a power station, and the thermal had sent us skyward, I have never been so frightened in my life!

Hugh then bought Biggin Hill Motorcycles, the motorcycle side of Dawnier Motors, a Skoda dealer. The purchase included quite a few new Suzuki and CZ machines. Biggin Hill was home to a lot of people who worked for the press and members of the police force; both well paid but always pleaded hard up, they liked their economy motorcycling, hence the CZ. I was put in charge. It very quickly became obvious that, instead of ordering any spares from Suzuki, or CZ, Dawniers just 'borrowed' bits from their new stock. Dave Hamilton, formerly of Mocheck was recruited as mechanic. Not a single machine was saleable, there were points missing, brake pads and shoes, cables. The situation was amicably solved by the previous owners, but it took Dave an awfully long time to get the bikes to a saleable condition. The Met Police had a finance company to assist its purchases, and we were able to join its supplier list, which helped get the new 'old' stock out of the door. I was there for about 18 months, before I moved back to this island I now call home; I have now lived here longer than on the 'adjacent island.'

I used to ride a Suzuki B100P to work at BHM. One day whilst going through the lanes near West Wickham, I encountered a Morris Minor being driven rather randomly by a member of the opposite sex, on my side of the road. She clattered into me, the bike went flying one way and I found myself astride her (locked) front wheel. We stopped and I extricated myself without any damage, but she was in a right state; if she had let that brake off, I could have been in a bigger mess!

PETER GALE

Green Velos are quite rare, but I often passed one going in the opposite direction whilst I was living at Mitcham, I was on my swinging arm 1955 MAC model, bought from Stuart Lines of the Devon and Cornwall Centre, the one which passed me was a c1953 rigid MAC with Velo teles. I often wondered who it was. Whilst riding in the trial at the Festival of a 1000 Bikes at Brands Hatch, this chap came up and introduced himself as Peter Gale, who lived in Biggin Hill – he was the green MAC man. When I moved back to the Island we lost touch, until one day at a Vintage club trial at Little London, he came and re-introduced himself; he had also moved to the Island. Peter and his friend Bill Baxter had ridden the Manx Two Day trial for many years, being probably the oldest competitors. He had a trials Cub which we occasionally shared at VMCC events. Peter was not quite of pensionable age when he moved across, so he lived very frugally until that big day came.

RAY KNIGHT

For 1970, I was helping Ray Knight at the TT. That year, Ray had borrowed the Boyer of Bromley 500-mile winning Triumph Daytona, ridden by Dave Nixon and Peter Butler the previous year. Stan Shenton had told Ray that the engine was tired, he couldn't guarantee it would last a lap or a race. This was the era of the Le Mans start: Ray ran across, I was holding the bike, his leg came over the saddle, hit the kickstarter and was gone. Who needs an electric start!

It was perceived to be a bit of an oil burner, so we had a plan. When he came in for fuel, I had the petrol filler in the left hand, and a quart jug of oil in the right, I gave him the filler, then ran round the other side, took the top off the (well smoky) oil tank, and poured it all in. It was either going to be enough, or it was going to go bang. As it was, there was enough lubricant in the engine for Ray to have a good scrap on that last lap with Gordon Pantall, even down to a bit of fairing rubbing at Hillberry, but Gordon beat Ray for second place by 0.04 of a second. The race was won by Frank Whiteway (Crooks Suzuki) with the scrapping Triumphs second and third. There was little trace of oil in the tank at the finish!

Being an ace blagger and tester of bikes, Ray had the use of a Honda 750 for the 1974 Formula One that had been used by Bill Smith at Daytona. It had been clocked at 174mph on the banking, but it must have left a great deal of horsepower provenance on that side of the water, as it barely reached 130 on the Island. It might have performed fine out in the US of A, but it was an absolute sod to start in Douglas. We were staying on Peel Road that year, the number of times Ray had to push down Bank Hill by the railway station was more than enough. Race day, it took a hissy fit and wore out marshals and spectators as far as Governors Bridge and back, as they endeavoured to get it to fire up, just before the start. In the end, someone made the comment "That bike didn't want to be ridden." It was a wasted effort as Ray had a rare non-mechanical dnf when he slid to earth at Braddan Bridge. I think he was glad to see the back of that one!

I was with Ray at Snetterton, when he was the first UK racer to use Bridgestone tyres for racing. There were a few ribald comments that day, but their attitude changed after Ray wiped the floor with them!

Ray has forgiven me for finding him his only 'stroker ride in the TT. I was chatting to Dennis Macmillan at his bike shop, and said that Ray was looking for bikes. Dennis' son Ricky was starting racing on an LC, so Dennis offered, and Ray accepted it for the 1982 Formula Two TT. It was a 'nippy' little thing: it nipped up three times on the opening lap, Ray quietly parked it at the pits to save any further damage and never repeated the 'stroker folly.

HARRY LONG

The very mention of Harry Long's name brings a smile to all who have ever met him. Harry and his Gold Star are legendary, he built it from bits, the Goldie head cost him the princely sum of 17 shillings and sixpence. The barrel – the casting had a crack in it, and if you turned it upside down, the liner fell out. Yet despite all this, it was damned quick bike for its class in Vintage racing. I well remember the first Manx Grand Prix he rode in, the 1984 Classic Senior. The bike was a bit of a 'Torrey Canyon,' leaking oil everywhere, so we purchased a large lump of carpet felting, and I spent a couple of hours on my back fashioning a 'nappy' that stretched from the front of the engine, right back and up almost to the seat, with a couple of slots for the chain.

I was watching at Governor's Bridge that day, all was going well. On the last lap, he appeared to shut off well before the line. I found him and the gang in the paddock afterwards, a beaming Harry dressed in his shorts. "What do you think of that dear boy?" he said, pointing to the Goldie. Hanging from the throttle cable was the big Amal GP, and half the inlet manifold: it had snapped by the police station and he'd coasted to the finish, shades of Reg Armstrong breaking his primary chain as he won the 1952 Senior TT.

Another time the top of the GP carb came off, the threads were, shall we say, a little 'worn.' It was secured by a piece of fence wire by spectators, which lasted the race. Harry's bikes were never pretty; one year the gang set to and polished the mudguards and generally sorted it out. When going up for pre-race scrutineering, David Harding, chief scrutineer, passed it and said, "New bike, Harry?"

One of our friends, Geoff Brandon had been bitten by a dodgy meat pie on the way to the Island, he fell quite ill and was transferred to Nobles with salmonella (sepsis). Me and Harry went to see him, he was as white as the sheets, it was only his bloodshot eyes that gave him away. Because of the infection, we had to wear gowns and hoods, one of our mates reckoned we looked like Burke and Hare on a mission! Geoff was successfully treated and allowed home.

Harry competed in Europe quite a bit with the BSA, Velo and Rudge, and was welcomed wherever he went. If you said, "Your leg's fallen off, Harry" he just laughed! Harry passed away in July, 2018, leaving many people with happy memories of 'The Laughing Chinaman'.

DAVE MASTERS

I have known Dave Masters since my Arthur Lavington days, he lived close by us at Croydon. Always a Velo Fellow, Dave wrote and illustrated three books chronicling the Velocette machines, even the only known Veloce car, built in 1908. Dave has also written *The Fiery Wheel*, a book chronicling the motorcycling life of Canon Basil Hart-Davies, better known in motorcycle circles as 'Ixion' who wrote many tales of his record-breaking pioneering rides in "Occasional Comments" in *The Motor Cycle* magazine, including holding the End-to-End record and riding the TT. Dave tracked down a 1913 veteran inlet-over-exhaust Veloce, which he rides in the Sunbeam MCC's Pioneer Run. (The name was changed to Velocette when Veloce built the small two-stroke models – although the word veloce is Italian for fast, the suffix 'ette', means small in French).

ROGER ASHBY

One year, I was unable to take my ride at the Arbuthnot Trial, so Roger Ashby took my Triumph 3HW on the event. The *Trials and Motocross* newspaper used a photo of him, but they captioned it as yours truly, from the programme. It was the only time he had his picture in the press, but was not given the credit!

On his first ride at the Classic Manx, on Richard Pelham's 7R, I was viewing at Braddan Bridge. Most riders came by in numerical order on the first lap, but Roger was a long way down already, and the bike stuttered into view. "Mag's gone," he said. I wasn't so sure, so I said in a loud voice if we can get the bottom carb nut off, it might be a blocked main jet. A few seconds later, a spanner mysteriously dropped out of the sky. Getting the jet out, yes, it was blocked and cleaned out, replaced: it was a working 7R again. Every lap through we got the thumbs up from Roger. On the last lap he was closely accompanied by the Roads Open car, but they held back and he got a finish. His face was a picture when I found him and the crew in the beer tent after the race!

During practice for the Classic Senior MGP another year, Roger was riding a G45 twin-cylinder Matchless. Pressing on past Ginger Hall, the whole clutch assembly came off and disappeared over the hedge. To this day, that clutch has never been found, the centrifugal force of the assembly must have sent it miles away.

Roger fancied riding the Classic TT on the Southern 100 course one year, and he asked if we could film the course for him. So we borrowed neighbour Rene's DAF and made the film, but before sending it, we spliced just a few seconds of an Electric Blue film intro onto it, I would have liked to have seen his (and his wife's) face at that split second!

ROY DAVIS

Former WWII bomber crew Roy had a garage full of MAC bits here on the Island, mainly swinging-arm models. He asked if I could make him one for VMCC runs. We used two mismatched crankcase halves, and a crankshaft from another engine, it was a real mix-and-match. Do you know what, it was the sweetest running MAC I had ever ridden!

NICK PAYTON, AND VELO BITS AND PIECES

When I left for the Island, I passed all my garage full of Velo stuff to Nick Payton. Nick had joined the workforce at Geoff Dodkin whilst I was there, he was a very capable bike fettler and long-time Velo fan. He is now one of the acknowledged experts in the Veloce field, and runs his business from home, Payton Place, in Colliers Wood. When I first knew him it was like a student squat, I couldn't think how many lived at that Colliers Wood house. I am sure I passed on a Venom to Nick with the reg 194 NMP, which just happens to be his initials.

Nick rode the Classic Manx Grand Prix on three occasions, finishing every time, and winning the trophy for the first machine to VMCC standards to finish.

One night, he was out riding his Thruxton when all forward motion ceased. He thought the inlet valve had dropped in, but when he went to pick it up, they were loading it into a van when they noticed the sparkplug hanging from its lead!

CHRIS 'SKID' ROWE

Some time after our meeting at Place Manor, Cornwall, 'Skid' Rowe, Fran and family came to live on the Island. Engineering-wise, he would tackle anything. I well remember his go-kart, fitted with a 500 BSA A7 twin engine, thundering round the field behind E B Christian's White Hoe depot, where he was foreman fitter. It was deadly, the only way to stabilise the thing was to fill the tyres with water.

His invitation to join EB's staff came an unusual way. During the TT one year, his car developed an issue, so he asked if he could sort it at EB's workshop, David Christian was so impressed by his skill, he offered him a job!

He would assist anybody with bike repairs and modifications, his garage was always full of bodies and bikes in the evenings. Well, almost anybody. We were working one evening when this fella came walking up the drive. The chap concerned had been a capable TT rider, but had questionable ethics. Chris uttered a short phrase, which indicated some sort of sexual direction to leave, and without breaking a step the chap turned 180 degrees on his heels and left.

We held Velo Club nights at the Rowe's house in the Strang, one memorable night we were playing music (possibly the 1812 Overture) that loud, I had to sit on the speaker to stop it waltzing across the room.

Chris' son Martin took to four wheels, becoming the British Rally Champion in 1998, and now works for the Subaru Rally development team in Canada. I met Martin again briefly when he came over for Skid's funeral, which was exceedingly well-attended.

PHIL NEWMAN

Yet another TT/MGP stopover to reach our little rock in the Irish Sea is Phil Newman. Racer, trials rider, biker and all-round adventurer, Phil is worthy of a book on his own. He is well known as the last person to ride a rigid frame machine (BSA Gold Star) in the 1984 Junior Classic Manx Grand Prix; he finished 29th (of the 33 finishers), riding under his step-father's name Neumüller.

He rode in the first Classic Club race meeting at Donington, his was the only rigid bike there that day, and he balloted No 1 on the grid for its first ever race.

Phil's overland expeditions are legendary; he remembers riding through the Khyber Pass. He found a pair of Germans, one of whom had forgotten which side of the road he should be driving on, and had head-butted a lorry, causing the front rim of his BMW to go egg-shaped. The lorry driver fastened the wreckage to the side of his truck and took them back to the frontier, where Phil stripped the wheel out, bashed the rim as near round he could, then rebuilt it so they could ride it to civilisation and get a new rim. The Khyber Pass is not a place to stay overnight!

He has ridden over the Khardung La, a mountain pass in the Ladakh region of the Indian state of Jammu and Kashmir, but on a Bullet this time. He used to winter in India for many years, but in winter 2017-18 he went to New Zealand with a home-built fold-up pushbike as transport, riding over 1500 miles on it.

He also camped under the Buddha statues carved into the cliffs at the Bamyan valley in the Hazarajat region of central Afghanistan. These have since been destroyed by the Taliban.

Phil's BSA B31 has well over 280,000 miles under its wheels, including an overland trip to Australia, where he worked for a few years on a geological survey. He recently went on a trip to the Arctic Circle on it. He and Chris Wallis have done two trips to the Orkneys, the first to take in the war history, the second to take in Orkney's archaeological heritage.

He used to buy Jaguar cars, take them to America and sell them for a bagful of dollars, and then enjoy the rewards until the money ran out, when he would come home and repeat the exercise.

Phil shares my passion for punching paper with pieces of hot lead, and was one of the Island's leading black-powder shooters. In 2015, he was selected for the Manx Squad at the Island Games, in Jersey. He duly won the Gold Medal for the 25-metre Black Powder Individual Final and finished fourth in the Pairs Final with Martin Cowley.

THOMAS ARTHUR CORLETT AND ROBIN CORLETT

I was introduced to Tommy Corlett by a mutual friend. Tommy lived at the School House, Dreemskerry, on the way out of Ramsey to Laxey. The Manx author Hall Caine was once the teacher at this school. The property did not have running water or electricity when I first met Tommy, he used water butts and an old JAP generator to provide his six-volt lighting. You sat there until it was quite dark before switching them on, then six volts was quite sufficient. Tommy and family used to live at Beaconsfield Tower, a windmill on the outskirts of Ramsey (now a retirement home). He and his father would repair anything mechanical, and also charge accumulators for people's radios. Tommy senior was once the owner, bought secondhand, of an Eadie Quadricycle, registration MN 22, one of the earliest Manx-registered vehicles. The Eadie was a fore-runner of Royal Enfield.

The Corlett family were always mad keen on photography, the School House (now owned by his son Robin) is packed with piles of photo albums; if you took a photo out, everyone has been annotated on the back with date, place taken, people and, if there was a bike, it would contain Tommy's comments about them. Tommy rode an Ivy sidecar in the early 1920s, and was the first person to ride to the summit of Snaefell in a sidecar. The early Ramsey Motorcycle Club (no relation to the modern sporting club) held its first event, a hillclimb, up the road by Ballaglass Glen. Tommy won that on an Ivy, with first prize of a mantle clock, presented to him by Pa Norton who was on the Island as a spectator for the TT at that time. The clock is still in the house.

I recall that Tommy said he was asked by double TT-winner Tom Sheard if he ever fancied riding in the TT. "I'm not a racer," was his reply. "Neither am I," said Tom, "but we both know which way the road goes." In the '20s, as today, the locals would do a lap or two every weekend, although the course at that time was basically an unmade lane, with grass growing between the tracks.

Tommy also worked with Graham Oates on building the Aurora motorcycle, the only Manx-constructed machine. Many years later, Tommy and Robin were walking along Ramsey Quay as a scrap boat was being filled by George Young, the local scrap merchant. He was just about to throw the petrol tank of an Aurora on board, but handed it to Tommy saying, "Here, Tommy have this as a souvenir of your first job."

Robin still owns the tank, which will feature, together with Graham Oates' motorcycling history (first man to go trans-Canada in 1928, and the first to reach Churchill in Hudson Bay on a rubber-tyred vehicle, riding his Ariel outfit up the railway line in 1932, TT rider, ISDT gold medalist) in the Manx Museum's new Motorsport Gallery, due to be completed in 2020.

Tommy was for many years the engineer for the Ramsey Lifeboat, he was still living by himself at Dreemskerry into his 90s, and carried on riding his Honda 90 until nearly the end.

Tommy's son Robin has inherited all the family scrapbooks, photos and memorabilia. Robin was quite a rider in his day, too. He set off in 1977 to ride overland to Melbourne, Australia on a Bantam. When the bike failed in India, it would have cost a lot of money to leave it there, so it was taken across to Pakistan where he removed the number plates and abandoned it. Who knows, it may still be sitting on the dockside!

ELWYN ROBERTS AND GRAHAM HOULIHAN

Gotta be Welsh with a name like that! I have known Elwyn for about 50 years now, and he has been a link for me to the older racers. He knew many of the prewar riders, not just aces but anyone who raced bikes. When prewar works Norton rider John H 'Crasher' White passed on, his family entrusted his suitcase of trophies to Elwyn.

2020 should have been his 50th TT visit, but it was of course cancelled due to the Covid-19 pandemic. He admitted, "I didn't think I would miss it that much, but I do." Some years he has visited our blessed Isle three times, for the TT, Southern 100 and Manx.

Elwyn has a phenomenal collection of photographs signed by riders. In the past, when he sent a pic, it had been known for riders to just keep them; now, he sends three copies, one for the rider, and one each to be signed for Elwyn and his mate Graham Houlihan. I provide what pictures I can. Graham, who lives in Urbania, Italy, has the autograph of every rider who has scored a world championship point since the championship started in 1949. It has taken him all over the world to track down these signatures. The last signature to complete this mammoth task was that of Argentinian Jorge Kissling, who won his home Argentinian 500 Grand Prix in 1961 on a G50 Matchless, an event which most of the Continental Circus teams and riders did not go to. Graham had to visit Argentina, and Jorge's family, where they gave him his racing licence, with the all-important signature. Elwyn hopes to fly over to the Isle of Man for a quick visit later in 2020, if the Covid situation settles down.

THE SATURDAY CLUB

We had been out on a TT course charity run, they hold many of these throughout the year. A group of us ended up in a café, as you do. This took me back to all those years ago, when we frequented the Saltbox and other cafés on runs out. I suggested we meet on a Saturday morning at various venues around the Island. From a small gathering it grew, we sometimes had about 40 people there. It was not just for bikers, but for anyone with a motorcycle interest. Sadly, personalities clashed, and the group split into two, but it was great fun while it lasted. There is a similar gathering at the Ramsey Swimming Pool on a Friday morning, called the Old Farts Club, run by Andre Pedro Midwood, you just plonk yourself down and chat to whoever is sitting next to you. When I get back on two wheels, I will get out and join them.

new books • ebooks • apps • newsletter • special offers • gift vouchers
www.veloce.co.uk / www.velocebooks.com

Despatch riding

Dave Richmond, *Motorcycle Weekly*'s Road Riding reporter, arrives at the BMF Rally: he still has Panthers in his garage today!

The 'Front Line' Despatch Riding column for *Motorcycle Weekly*.

MOTORCYCLING WEEKLY, MARCH 4 1986 25

DESPATCH RIDING

Work in Sheffield?

THANKS for the great despatch riding column Bill.

I am writing because I am thinking of getting a job as a despatch rider in the near future. The only problem is that I live in Derbyshire and I don't know of any despatch companies in my area.

Do you know of any despatch companies in Derbyshire, Sheffield area that would be worth contacting for employment?

G. HODGKISS
Chesterfield, Derby.

I suggest you start by looking in the Yellow Pages directory for despatch companies in your area. However it is possible that a number of the columns might be able to give you specific contacts, or perhaps

FRONT LINE

with BILL SNELLING

Exclusive! The only weekly column for despatch riders

For Shuttle's sake – I'm being followed!

Road test:
BILL SNELLING
Photography:
PHIL MASTERS

Riding and evaluating the Sidewinder Shuttle for my Despatch Riding column in *Motorcycle Weekly*.

Living on the Island

Manxman Dennis Craine leads Peter Williams (Greeves) at Signpost Corner, 1965 Lightweight Manx Grand Prix. Dennis won, Peter was third.

Our house, as portrayed on a Gibsons jigsaw puzzle. It depicts the Kelly family who stayed there in the 1970s, together with their machines.

Jurby Airfield action: the Thruxton, built from spares in our Mitcham garage.

Nick Payton warms up my Thruxton, whilst Peter Kermode and myself get the Velo Metisse cracked up.

Giving the Thruxton some beans round the hangar section of the Jurby Airfield circuit.

Jurby Airfield: a rare occasion when I was leading Neil Kelly (Honda).

Bernie Lund (AJS) in the 1965 Junior TT. I worked for Bernie at Grand Prix Motorcycles in 1981.

Mates

A trials riding pal, biking journalist and ace blagger of bikes, Ian Kerr MBE on Bob Dowty's T20 Suzuki, on the TT parade lap.

The two Kens: Ken Blackburn, left, and Ken Law, astride his KSS with McCandless rear suspension, at the Niarbyl Bay Velo Rally.

The other MV in the 1967 Senior TT, apart from Ago! Hugh Evans and his BSA A50-engined MV.

Peter Gale and brother Bob with Peter's Norton on their race transporter, ready for the Knatts Valley Hillclimb.

Ray Knight watches as Ron May prepares 'Secondhand Rose' that Ray rode in the 1983 Formula One TT.

Ray Knight at Quarter Bridge on the smoky Boyers of Bromley T100.

Ray Knight on the Bill Smith Honda, which was a sulky starter and finally spat him off at Braddan Bridge, in the 1974 Formula 750 TT.

Ray Knight (Yamaha) on his only 'stroker TT. He has forgiven me for arranging this ride!

Harry Long cracks a joke (what else?) with the Scrutineers at the Manx Grand Prix.

Harry Long strikes trouble on my 3HW in the MCC Land's End Trial.

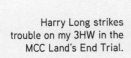

Two Veloce! Dave Masters and American Pete Young took part in the London to Brighton Run on their Veloce machines.

Manxman Bill Snelling weaves through a muddy section on board his 1941 Triumph 3HW.

Not me! Roger Ashby, who took my ride on the 3HW in the Arbuthnot Trial.

'Crashby' Roger Ashby waits to start a practice lap on Richard Pelham's 7R, Manx Grand Prix.

Nick Payton, fettling his Velo
at Payton Place.

Nick Payton at the Bungalow, 1986 Senior Classic Manx
Grand Prix.

Chris 'Skid' Rowe riding his Matchless at the Rushen Mines.

Phil Newman guides his BSA Gold
Star (named Bloodysaurus!) into
Governor's Bridge. It was the last
rigid frame machine to have been
ridden in the Manx Grand Prix, at the
1984 Junior Classic MGP.

Phil Newman reaches the summit of the Khardung La Pass in India.

It's Hell out there! Phil Newman and Orry Teare on their Arctic Circle trip, Hell Station, Norway.

Thomas Arthur Corlett and pet pooch in his dad's Eadie quadricyle. This was MN 22, the 22nd vehicle registered in the Isle of Man.

This is the Ivy Three that I bought from Alf Lawton in Castletown on 27th August 1923 for £30. She was one of the most likable bikes I ever had. She had been used as a practice machine in the 1921 T.T. practice period — by S.A. Newman & Co Ltd — the makers. 348 cc 3 port twostroke. 3 speed C & KS Sturmey Archer gear box, chain & belt transmission. Dripfeed lubrication. E.I.C magneto. Amac Carburetter 26 x 2¼ tyres. In 1924 (June)? I entered the Ivy for my very first competition, a Hill Climb at Ballaglass Glen. We tied for fastest time of the day & the old Ivy & I won on formular — a very nice brass clock. Tommy Corlett

Tommy Corlett with his Ivy on which he won the Ballaglass Hillclimb, the first event held by the Ramsey Motorcycle Club, 1924, and details on the rear of the picture.

Tommy Corlett with his first bike, a baby Triumph, and right, with his last bike, a Honda 50, which he was still riding in his 90s.

Robin Corlett, about to set off to ride overland to Australia, on a BSA Bantam.

Competing

Competing at my first MCC trial. I am on the KSS-MAC at the first hairpin on Fingle Bridge in the 1964 Exeter Trial.

Saltbox and Velo Club friends Pete and Beryl Redman, with Rod Weight.

The Flintstone as bought in Portsmouth, with the fibreglass tank. Note the boxes of spares festooned around the garage!

Pretty it ain't! The Flintstone, my double MCC championship-winning Velo, posing against a Manx drystone wall.

The Flintstone still with standard footrests, and also with Del's tweaked silencer.

Riding the Flintstone up the Crackington Haven section on the MCC Land's End Trial. (Courtesy Pete Redman)

Adrian Pirson just about to ride off after buying the Flintstone. Behind him is John Pocklington and Pete Miles.

Lieutenant Governor Sir Laurence New and Joey Dunlop at the TT prize-giving, 1986

Morini-mounted at Crackington Haven in the MCC Land's End Trial.

The Camel Train at the end of the Exeter Trial: yours truly, Paul Evans and Benjy Straw.

'Short-portly' tackling Simms on the Triumph 3HW in the MCC Exeter Trial. You needed those handlebar muffs in January!

A brew stop by the Lady Bower on the MCC Edinburgh Trial.

After a whoopsie on Bamford Clough in the MCC Edinburgh Trial. Proving that the BMW R80 RT is not a suitable trials machine!

The 3HW on an MCC Edinburgh trial section.

A baby, baby Triumph! Taking care not to crush it, this ace small replica was on show at the Belle Vue motorcycle show.

(continues page 97)

COMPETING

MCC TRIALS AND TRIBULATIONS
THE FLINTSTONE
Arthur Lavington rode the MCC trials for many years, it was following these that gave me a taste to compete.

The Motor Cycle Club was formed in 1901, one of the earliest motorcycle clubs to be formed. In 1904 they inaugurated the long-distance event, which was probably called a 'reliability run' in those days, as the vehicles were still quite primitive, and with the state of the 'byways' you could not really call them roads!

The first MCC trial I rode was the 1964 Exeter Trial on a KSS-engined MAC, bought from a mate Jock Hopson. I only got as far as Fingle Bridge, where I gave the clutch a bit of a roasting (even though we had geared down) and then punctured at the top of Fingle's myriad hairpins. I rode it back to the Exeter control, where I snoozed in the car and Dad repaired the puncture – I had no stamina in those days!

A more suitable mount was needed, so we found a Scrambler-framed MSS project down in Southampton. It was clean, tidy, and at the right price. We filled Dad's Mini Countryman with the bike and hauled it back home. It was an unfinished project, it had a BSA-style fibreglass tank fitted, but I found the proper Endurance tank, based on a Valiant tank, and we proceeded to make it fit for purpose. With a red frame, and assembled from Velo bits from all ages, we christened it 'Flintstone,' a name that stuck. As the MCC trials run through the night, it had a full lighting set. In its early days, it was Miller-lit, not the best system ever invented (the lamp manufacturer Joseph Lucas used to be called 'Prince of Darkness,' a name I feel more suited to the Miller). In the later years, I purchased one of the first Criterion alternator sets; what a revelation, you could roll the throttle off on hairpins and still see where you were aiming for. The standard footrest layout puts too much weight on the front wheel, so after much experimentation balancing the bike on bathroom scales, the Flintstone was fitted with rear sets which gave the correct weight bias to the rear wheel. A high pipe was fitted, with a standard fishtail; this looked a bit cumbersome, so a mate from the Saltbox Club, Del Whitton, cut six inches out of the middle and welded it back together again.

The Flintstone was an ideal mount; in 1966 we won the MCC motorcycle championship with two first-class awards and a second, including winning the

Edinburgh-Derbyshire outright. In 1967 we repeated the championship win, the first double-winner (to that date). I could have had a Triple that year, but just dabbed out of the 'free foot' area on the stop-and-restart on Bluehills, the last section of the event. In 1968, I finally gained a Triple, awarded to those who claimed a first class in all three events, the Exeter, Land's End and the Edinburgh, (confusingly now held in Derbyshire). Of the three, I really liked the Edinburgh-Derbyshire, it was an area I only rode once a year. I was pipped for the Club championship for the third time on special test times.

One Boxing Day I decided to visit the Devon and Cornwall branch of the Velo Club's meet at Fingle Bridge, near Exeter. It was snowing hard but the roads didn't seem too bad when I left home. Near Thruxton race circuit, I was following in the wheel tracks of a snow clearer; the visor had become mucky because I was wiping it with a Barbour mitt, so pulled over to clear it. I slid into a ditch, which flicked the gearlever up and disarranged the operating pawl inside the box. I had always carried a good selection of spanners, so I was able to extract the mainshaft, remove the gears and re-install the pawl. I did not carry on with that trip, I retraced my steps to Mitcham.

I was out trail riding one day at Box Hill near Dorking with mates Pete, Beryl and Chris Bryant. Cresting a rise, a protruding tree branch neatly broke my left shoulder blade and held me there as the Flintstone went from between my legs. It stopped, and to add insult to injury, it fell against the tree I was hanging off and severely dented the petrol tank. I got home okay, and got strapped up, but the same week, as I was walking down to the pub (not back from), I tripped over a kerb and re-broke it!

In 1968, my 21st birthday coincided with the Land's End; the Saltbox had taken over a caravan site near Tintagel. I guessed the amber liquid may have flowed that night. After finding the right caravan (they all look the same in a purple haze), someone cracked a funny and I sat and laughed for about 4 hours, in the morning my midriff was sore!

I sold the Flintstone to Adrian Pirson, then Chairman of the Velo Club (for £300). Adrian also won an MCC triple on it, and later came to live here on the Island. In 2017, I got a surprise email from Adrian to say he was selling it, and would I like it back? With leg and hip joint problems and living on a pension, I declined the offer. I would make an educated guess that he would have asked a bit more than the original £300 that I sold it to him for. It had also stood in an unheated garage for over 30 years, so it would have needed a total refurbishment, well out of the scope of this pensioner. I heard in December 2018 that someone had bought all of Adrian's bikes, so it's likely the Flintstone may have a new lease of life.

I later rode the MCC trials on a rigid-frame Velo MAC with an MDD frame and gearbox, this had rear-mounted footrests and a very low first gear, ideal for the sections. It was obviously not competitive, but I enjoyed the ride, managing to pick up a third-class award in the Edinburgh-Derbyshire.

Through the friendship with Benjy Straw, I had a few outings on Morini Camels, and also Paul Evans' Morini special that was so high I could barely touch the floor when astride – no good for the many stop-and-restart tests on these trials. Paul now runs the Internal Fire Museum of Power at Tanygroes, a few miles north of Cardigan in Wales.

My last MCC mount was a 1941 ex-WD 3HW Triumph, fitted with trials tyres and a cobby high-level pipe. On this I managed a third-class in the Edinburgh in 1988; even beating my mate who was riding a Honda Transalp. Of all the bike events I have ridden, I miss the MCC trials most of all.

One year, Simon Fenning of Motovecchia fancied riding the Land's End, he had a really trim Yamaha, possibly XT model. On the run down south, it was not running like it should. He struggled on, but it was getting to be hard work. We spent some time looking for the problem. The bike had started out immaculate, it had been cleaned specially (we didn't take that line ourselves). "When you cleaned it, did you protect the air cleaner?" I asked. There was a strangled "Ye-e-es," he took the seat off, and removed the plastic bag that kept the air filter dry. It ran perfectly after that!

THE TAPERING LOO
One of the refuelling stops on the Land's End Trial was at a garage in the Devon village of South Moulton. It was an interesting experience if you were caught short, and needed to use the facilities. The loo was a door's width, but tapered to about the width of the porcelain. One had to enter, turn round, and back into use Thomas Crapper's invention. Wearing all the layers to keep the night's cold out, it was quite a struggle!

PINNED TO THE FENCE
One Exeter trial, Mum and Dad were following the route down west, and, at a particularly sharp corner, Dad spotted something odd out of the corner of his eye. He stopped the car and went back to check. A competitor had misjudged the corner, hit the bank, somersaulted over the bars, and had become pinned to the fence by his Barbour jacket, unable to move. Dad held him up while Mum undid his jacket and he slid out of it. I think he was a relation to Jack Pouncy, but could not swear to it. Shaken but not stirred, he retrieved the bike and carried on. One lucky fella!

My mate Ian Kerr and his Met Police mates were riding the Exeter with us, and I was on the '41 Triumph 3HW. Because of low gearing, the old bike and 'short portly' pilot, we rode everywhere at 46mph, with Ian glued to my high-level exhaust, keeping the winter chill at bay! They kindly bought me lunch at the end as a reward for my trail-blazing.

Mum and Dad always followed the MCC events in a car, and could often be found brewing up in a lay-by. The Met Police team could smell a teapot from miles away, and they would normally be supping away before we arrived – their Triumph Saints were a bit quicker than the sludge pumps we were riding.

On an Edinburgh trial, just by the Lady Bower reservoir, we knew where they were, although we couldn't see their car, the queue of bikes in the lay-by gave away their location.

Another year, Mum bought a tray of barely time-expired Mr Kipling individual fruit pies at a bargain price (a penny each, I seem to remember). I think everyone on the Exeter that year existed on them!

One year, the Met boys on their Triumphs came past us in haste. Just round the corner was a large green triangle, the first member had gone left, the second right, the third, Ron Hawkins was sprawled in the middle. He had injured a knee, so abandoned the trial, and rode home – when he got there he leant on the horn button to get his family help him off his bike.

THE 1987 EDINBURGH-DERBYSHIRE

In 1987, I had entered the Edinburgh-Derbyshire, but was without a suitable mount. I was despatch riding at the time for CCL, Concorde Couriers Ltd of Kingston, on a BMW R80RT. I had decided to follow the trial, but on getting to the start, my mates persuaded me to compete. I had to tape over the company's logo, and was advised to remove the panniers so that if (when) I footed, I wouldn't break an ankle on them, Jack Pouncy took them to the finish for me. The night run from Coventry to Derbyshire was most enjoyable, with the RT's fairing keeping the cold at bay. But many of the sections were a different matter. Road tyres, gearing and mud don't mix, though the sandy ones weren't that bad. I recall climbing Millstone Edge, a rocky outcrop near Ashburton. I came to a hairpin and whistled round it – road gearing makes trail riding exciting! As I flew past, I spotted Geoff Wilson, BMW club chairman standing there and, as I made a fast exit, I heard him utter an expletive.

Bamford Clough is a long, rock-strewn hill starting from the village of Bamford, near Castleton and finishing high on the moors. It had a dry surface, so I thought I stood a chance of reaching the top. I was making good progress until, about halfway up, the bugger turned sharp left on me and mounted a low stone wall. Methinks, "About time to bail out", which I did in great haste. Getting up, I was confronted with an R80RT sitting on the wall upside down, wheels pointing skywards. Fortunately, there was a long drop the other side of the wall, and the screen was completely undamaged. All my gear, which had tumbled out the fairing pockets, was strewn across the field. Then came the fun of righting the machine; it would be fair to say that getting it back on its wheels with the aid of spectators and marshals, we put more scratches on the tank and fairing. As we were at the steepest point of the hill, there was no chance of carrying on, so we had to head back down again. Road tyres, high gearing and brakes that locked the wheels when you touched them made for an exciting descent. Add to this there was a scutch of riders across the track, waiting for their turn to climb. Frantic gesticulations allowed me a passageway through the crowd, and I just managed to pull up before we hit the main road! As a postscript; the mechanic who serviced the Concorde BMW fleet was rather unhappy with a less-than-pristine machine that I took back, but my bacon was saved by writing of my exploits in *Motorcycle Sport* magazine: Graham Koster, the boss of Concorde was an avid '*Sport* reader, and I gave the company a good plug in the article. But they never let me forget about trialling an unsuitable Beemer. I finished the trial, but well outside the awards, then headed off to Belle Vue for the bike show there. I was writing the despatch riding column for *Motorcycle Weekly* at that time, and had arranged to meet some of the staff there. I was perched on a half-scale Triumph which made me look even larger than I am! I have a photo of the Bamford prang, but only after we had righted the bike.

I was riding in company with Benjy Straw and other Morini members on their V-twins. One sticky hill, it may have been Putwell, I sussed that the grass could have the potential for some grip, and managed to clean it. I am afraid Benjy's Camel lived up to its name and bit him! He had to go to hospital but joined us all at a Chinese restaurant in Buxton with the naff name of Double Luck, but by gum the banquet they laid on was superb!

THE BREAKFAST FACTORY, MINEHEAD

The Land's End Trial seemed to be punctuated by an endless number of breakfast stops. One such was at Minehead. To save countless bikes and cars traversing this sleepy town at Easter, the check point was at the Butlin's Holiday Camp, on the outskirts of town. We were then bussed into town, where provision was made for breakfast at a large fish and chip shop. You have to bear in mind that they were expecting to cater for 300+ competitors and passengers. To do this they had filled the heated cabinets, normally carrying fish, pies and possibly saveloys, with seemingly hundreds of sausages, eggs, bacon, a myriad of pots full with baked beans, and an assembly line of toasters. Heaven help a vegetarian who rode these events!

THE SMOKY MAC

The trials MAC had a habit of sticking the inlet valve open, so I always took a small tin of Redex with me. On one occasion, nearing Bluehills Mine towards the end of the Land's End trial, it stuck open. I took the plug out, dropped an amount of Redex through the hole, replaced the plug and tried to bump start it. After a few seconds it burst into life, and I was immediately engulfed in smoke. It was smoking out of the timing cover, between the crankcase halves; the barrel and head were also engulfed, as was the chain case, but it did the trick! It was smoking so hard that competitors came back, expecting a conflagration, not just someone standing amidst a huge cloud of Redex smoke.

One Land's End Trial, round about the Lynton area, we came up behind a

1920s bike, which was riding on acetylene lights (it could have been Phil Heath, not absolutely sure). I was amazed at the bright light that the carbide emitted, as we climbed towards Exmoor.

Another year, when it snowed over the top, we were riding in deep snow when a snowdrift moved under a mate's wheels: he had ridden up the back of a sheep that was sleeping on the road!

Beggars Roost was one of the first hills on the Land's End. I only failed it once when the Norton 500T I was riding dropped out of gear. As I stopped, I was suddenly aware there were hundreds of spectators there – an eerie sight at around midnight. When charging on, you couldn't usually see anybody. The local postman used this road every day, but it could still take marks off the unwary. The same trials sections were used by car competitors as well, these days the 'classic' bikes do not have to contend with all the stop and restart tests as in my day.

TRIALS: VELO, DOUGLAS AND VAUXHALL

On the Island we had knocked together a rigid trial MAC from bits and pieces, 'Skid' Rowe made a pair of fork links to raise the ground clearance. By this time Tiger Cubs etc, were being used, but it was still bloody good fun. When Vintage trials started on the Island, there was one bike, Bob Thomas' Douglas Light 500, and about six riders: more of that bike later. Bob Thomas and Roy Davis always had a cuppa ready at the end of an event.

A posse of Manxies decided to enter the Talmag one year – we crammed as many as we could into a Transit. As well as the four bikes and six passengers, there was a 45 gallon drum of diesel that had been 'donated' to the cause! The Talmag is held on MoD land at Long Valley, near Aldershot, with sections laid out for different classes. The girder forkers rode the sidecar sections.

After passing the Velo on, I was loaned the Bob Thomas Douglas Light 500, a 1931 500cc in-line twin built to take advantage of lower tax for lighter machines (they ought to bring that back today!). It was the same as had been used by every entrant all those years earlier, the rear tyre was rock hard even without any air in it, no attempt to get more ground clearance other than an inch plate to raise the engine in the frame.

It was a bit of a beast to ride, but an unusual beast. I recall riding it in the first Manx Two Day Classic Trial in 1984: a bit ambitious to say the least, I think I three'd maybe four sections over the two days, one or two I rode through the start gate and back out again, but at least I can say finished, even if I could barely walk for two days afterwards.

One of the quirks of the Dougie was its issues with water; if you lifted the crankshaft mounted clutch in deep water, two things happened: first, the clutch hydraulicked and you lost drive; second, because of the narrowness of the petrol tank, a plume of water came up, temporarily blinding you in one orb, whilst making you rather uncomfortable a few feet lower! A few subtle holes drilled in the clutch plate resolved the clutch slipping issue, I had to put up with the discomfort!

I very often wore a Steam Packet guernsey and a peaked Steam Packet porter's cap whilst riding the Dougie at the Talmag. The Light 500 was more competitive at the Talmag, but its lack of ground clearance was always an issue: where you would normally drop over a ridge, you had to gun it to get the back wheel on the edge, being a very long-wheelbase machine, which did cause some consternation for spectators and officials. I well remember one section where the moderns had to do the twiddly bits, while sidecars and girders just rode the gulley. The Dougie with its open pipes sounded like a Triumph twin, so one of the spectators heard it, thought it to be a modern and stood in 'our' section. I was giving it big dixie up the hill, and rounded a bend to find him in my way: he was legging it up a 'very' steep bank, but not getting very far as I whistled under his bum! I guess if I hit him I could have claimed a baulk!

On one occasion I was about to enter a section when the bike stopped dead; the oil pipe had been pulled off going through some bushes, and it suffered a light seizure. We let things cool down, and it seemed fine, so we free-wheeled down a couple of slopes, put the plugs back in and carried on. Another time the mag got stinking hot and seemed to have given up the ghost, but a dowsing of R Whites lemonade soon had it running again.

With the wintry weather at Talmag time, with only one carb and long induction pipes, it was hard to warm up in the morning. You would run it for ten minutes before it conked out, with ice forming on the manifold, leave it for another ten minutes and start again. After about four sessions like this, it was red hot, and then stayed so throughout the day. I was warming it up one year when a guy on an Ariel rode up, looked at it and said, "That ought to be in my museum." Who did he think he was – Sammy Miller? Yes!

The Dougie's owner, Bob Thomas, lived at Milntown, home of Sir Clive Edwards, the youngest baronet at that time. When Sir Clive was enlisted in the army, he had to learn to ride a bike. The serving officer pointed to Bob and said, "And he will teach you." They became firm friends; Bob used to prepare Sir Clive's cars, including his six-wheeled HRG for hillclimbs and sprints like Shelsey Walsh. Despite their both passing on, The Milntown Trust, which now runs Milntown House, on the outskirts of Ramsey, still houses a great number of Sir Clive's cars and Bob's bikes and is open to the public. Sir Clive was the life and soul of the party, the ruder the joke you told, the better he liked it. "What comes out of a man's penis when he makes love? – The wrinkles!" Bob had a bike shop in Bicester before moving to the Island.

In 1993, a trio of us headed down to Beaulieu Motor Museum, to collect the Freddie Dixon Douglas banking sidecar, to display at the 70th anniversary of its winning the very first Sidecar TT. The sidecar is owned by Beaulieu, the bike was reconstructed by Bob. Beaulieu has an amazing array of vehicular transport down there, plus some amazing interactive rides: the one featuring the rally car, which nearly threw you out of the seat was the main one I remember. Coming back, we stopped at the big transport café on the A5 at Cannock. The steak pie was magnificent, but whether it was that which led to my first bout of incredible gout for the rest of the journey, we will never know. Every time the clutch was dipped, it was like being speared! And the M6 was full of roadworks, stop-start-stop-start for miles, or in my case stop-ouch-start-ouch!

The bike caused amusement as we wheeled it into the scrutineer's bay behind the regular outfits. Just prior to the start of the first Sidecar TT for '93, during the lunch break, we quietly wheeled the machine onto the grid and left it there. Peter Kneale, Manx Radio anchorman suddenly spotted it, he knew the significance of it. Perhaps in 2023 we can repeat it, as the machine is currently on the Island at Milntown House! I have a photograph of winners Dave Molyneux and Karl Ellison sitting on it in the winners' enclosure. Ian Kerr and I rode it down to the Vintage Club meeting at Castletown; even with my bulk it was so easy to crank it left and right.

Through my acquaintance with Bob Thomas, I was able to ride a unique motorcycle, the in-line Vauxhall four. Produced in 1922, when Vauxhall was thinking of breaking into the motorcycle scene, the engine was designed by Major Halford of Weslake, based on his aero engine experience. A lot of car manufacturers those days also made bikes, Sunbeam, Rover etc. Shaft-drive, it was something very special, and a great privilege to ride, albeit for a very short distance. Enough parts were made to produce three bikes, but we think only one was built.

The machine was in kit-form when Bob got it, and the wheels were missing: the previous owner had put them under the floor during the war, and forgotten them when he moved house. Bob had to knock on the door, explain the situation and ask if he could lift carpets and floorboards, to get his wheels – luckily they agreed! He contacted the people at Vauxhall to see if they had any plans etc, and he was sent a complete set of engineering drawings; within a few weeks of those plans being sent to Bob, the drawing office at Vauxhall burnt down! The tank was one of the missing parts, but Vauxhall got its apprentices to make a replica. The machine was low-geared, suitable for sidecar use, Bob rode a complete lap of the TT course in top gear. Another link to my motorcycling is that the Vauxhall had been ridden in the Land's End Trial.

HILLCLIMBS

My only hillclimb was at Wiscombe Park, near Exeter, c1966. I rode the Viper down from Mitcham, I was put up by Stuart Lines and together with Gordon Gurney, we had a banquet of a feast at a local Chinese. The hill is on the Wiscombe Estate, 1000 yards long, with hairpin bends and some long straights. The surface through the trees was mossy – off-putting at first, but did not make any difference to grip. *Motor Sport*'s Grand Prix journalist 'Jenks'

(Dennis Jenkinson) was there riding his Triumph-BSA. The hill is so narrow that some of the Formula 5000 cars barely have room to twitch off-line. I probably finished last, but it was an enjoyable day, even the weather was kind on the way home too.

THE ISDT
The International Trial was held on the Island three times, in 1965, 1971 and 1975, which meant that those years I visited the Island four times: TT, Manx, Southern 100 and ISDT. I was watching the '65 event up at Glen Auldyn, where there was a slippery wooden bridge. One competitor tumbled off while crossing it, his bike going into the river; the next chap was that close he ended up astride the rider, across his chest. These were the lightweights, 50 or 80cc. I went across and lifted the front end and the trapped chap crawled out, but as soon that front wheel hit terra firma, the trapee was off like a shot! That particular section eventually joined the TT course just above Guthrie's Memorial. Having seen the struggle the professionals had on it, I have never attempted it. It may not be a greenway, just land that permission had been granted to run the trial across.

TRAIL RIDING ON THE ISLAND
One evening, I fancied a run out and rode to St John's, to ride the Slieau Whallian track, which I had used many times, but always in a group. I was on the '41 Triumph 3HW. It had been raining hard, and at one spot, the footrests dug into the ground. I could not move forwards or back. It took me about three hours to extricate the bloody thing, and I never went trailing alone again after that.

On another ride, we were heading from Sky Hill to come out at the East Mountain Gate. My compatriots that day were Martin Goodey (RGS BMW) and Peter Gale (TL 125 Honda). At that time I was riding a TS185 Suzuki. When we hit the bog, Martin's Beemer sunk until the cylinders held it up, though we got it out with a struggle. Peter was OK on his little Honda, and then I tried to cross it on the Suzuki, giving it full welly as I charged at the bog. The front wheel dug in, the steed refused, but the rider was game! I exited over the handlebars and landed head first, at such a force that it pushed mud right into the helmet. I raised my head and the bog seemed to be alive – it was the only time in my life that I made the earth move!

The Island has many miles of unsurfaced roads, but the use of motocross type tyres which cut deep into the surface have caused great scars over the hills. The four-wheel-drive brigade do a lot of damage also, they thrive on getting stuck and have to winch each other out.

RACING
Because of my sometimes hairy-arse riding, it was suggested to me to try racing, so in late 1970, I bought a Viper Clubman for £50. Asking around, a

set of leathers was offered for £25 from John Battams, Chairman of the BSA Owners' Club. He must have been a big lad, because they were even too big for me!

Like most racers of that time, I took my brakes down to Joe Dunphy in Sydenham Road, Beckenham, South London to have the green AM4 linings fitted, his little red stickers were very much in evidence on brake plates in those days.

My first race was a Triumph Owners' Club High Speed Trial meeting at Lydden in 1971. These meetings were for road machines, solos and sidecars, and also catered for vintage machines. In addition to races, they ran half-hour trials. The flag dropped and you were set a number of laps, depending on the capacity of your machine; at Lydden it was 18 for a first class on a 350, 17 laps for a second-class. In addition to the Viper, I then owned the ex-works Roy Peplow 500 ISDT Triumph (106 CWD) that he had won Gold on in the International Six Days Trial on the Isle of Man in 1965. This I fitted with road tyres and gave it a good thrashing round the Kent circuit. Despite the larger capacity, I achieved the same number of laps on the 500 Triumph as on the Viper; I have always had a better feeling for riding singles than vertical twins, I got a second-class award on the Viper.

That evening, I was riding in a night road trial run by the Bexley Heath club: the Travellers Road Trial. I had a rigid Velo MAC for road trials, so Dad rode it down to Lydden, he then rode home on the Triumph. I made my way to the start of the trial, and won it! The trial finished at Johnson's Café, then home to bed after a full day of motorcycling. I later sold the Triumph to Saltbox friend Pete Winchester, who was going to use the engine in a Cheney Triumph, I am pleased to hear 106 CWD exists in its original format.

At my second Lydden meeting, we set off on the first event, when Bryan Clarke slid off his Venom at Pilgrim's, a few yards from the start. He was sliding down the track on his backside, legs akimbo, with my front wheel scant inches from his wedding tackle, and trying very hard not to ruin his chances. I slowed quicker than Bryan, I think he was grateful, must ask him!

The Viper carburettor float sprung a leak and sank at this meeting, during the lunch break I was trying to evaporate some of the fuel that entered it over our camping stove, it caused some concern from our fellow campers in the paddock – but it worked!

On another meeting, run by the Vincent Owners' club, going along the Park Straight at Cadwell, the Viper gave a rattle that was silenced when I pulled the clutch in – a top valve collar had broken allowing the exhaust valve to make intimate contact with the piston! It also pulled the valve guide down. The valve hit the piston flat, although it had an S-bend in the stem, it didn't do any further damage. The piston was cleaned and crack-tested, a new valve, guide and collar were fitted, and we were out racing the next weekend.

At another Cadwell meeting, one of the Velo lads fell off in practice, the bike catching fire. The circuit's owner Chas Wilkinson sought the owner of the crispy Velo, put a few folding notes into his hand and said, "Get it sorted, lad." You would not get that from the modern conglomerate circuit owners.

The Wilkinson family had owned the Cadwell Estate since 1934, and, before the war, allowed their sons and their mates to ride, and then race round their park. It was then part-paved before it became the full race circuit we know today. The first post-WWII race meeting on British soil was a two-day event at Cadwell Park at Easter 1946. It was estimated that 15,000 people packed round the three-quarter mile circuit, 20 deep to watch road racing restart.

Pat and I were visiting Horncastle in 2017 to meet Morton's Motorcycle Media archivist Jane Skayman and ad-lady Helen Martin. Cadwell was just a few miles up the road, so I just had to show Pat where my only racing success happened. It doesn't seem to have changed a lot in the intervening 30+ years, but the café is a bit bigger than the log cabin it used to be; we had been royally fed in Horncastle so I passed on the bacon baps this time.

Having added a Venom to the Viper, it gave me the chance of more rides. I used to ride the Viper in 500 events, and the Venom as a 501 in the unlimited events. One year, Nick Payton's bike suffered engine issues so he borrowed my Venom for a handicap race. Going through the Gooseneck, yellow flags were waving and there on its side was my Venom, with a very apologetic Nick getting to his feet! The tank was already in a bit of a state, but Nick added it to his collection for his racers, one side read 'ding' the other side 'bloody dong!' Our similar helmet un-designs are because I gave Nick my previous year's helmet when I bought a new one. After seeing what 'short portly' could do, he started racing too, becoming a top-flight runner in VMCC racing for many years.

In 1975, Nick and I teamed up for a British Formula Club 500km race, 250km on Saturday, 250km on Sunday. As you may know, Nick has a dicky left knee after hitting a tractor in Ireland, so he has to ride with an abbreviated forward footrest and use his heel on the brake. That day we presented the bike to the scrutineers with three footrests attached, and explained that they were "his, mine and ours!" We had a good ride until late on the first day, when a cam follower sheared. The motor was fitted with a polydyne cam, and it had given the followers a hard life. We pushed it into the paddock parc fermé expecting our race to be over. We were chatting with one of the officials and knowing that it could be repaired, she said: "Leave it in the shady corner, it might 'heal' itself." The paddock emptied as everyone headed for the pub or Harry Ramsden's chip shop. The tank was already loose, we whipped the timing cover off, took out the knackered cam followers and cams, refitted with a straight pair of push rods and, yes, it had healed itself, as forecast! It was quite a bit slower with a standard cam, but we got it to the finish. The next year Eunice Evans teamed with Nick on the Velo, that was a bit of change from her usual Honda 500 four.

In the mid-'70s, I bought a Thruxton-engined, Jim Lee-framed bike on the Island. Neil Kelly had raced one for L Stevens in the 1967 Senior Manx Grand Prix, but there is no way of knowing if it was this machine. I robbed the engine out and sold the chassis, as I had bought a Seymour Velo Metisse in the meantime. The engine was sent to Seymour's for race preparation. This engine was the one I used in the Avon series, as chronicled below.

I was racing with the British Formula Club for a few years, run by the very firm but fair hands of John and Joan Milligan. At one Lydden meeting, Dennis Macmillan was racing a quick 500 Ongar Honda Four in production and open races. He was known for his lightning starts in both classes, it was twigged on open races that he gave one step, hit the button and was off. For the second open race of the day, John Milligan produced a thimble which he taped over the start button; Dennis probably still won. The third race, he was off like a rocket again, he had transferred the start wire to the horn button!

Most of the following section came from an article I wrote for *Fishtail*, the Velo Club magazine, but have added further memories.

RAVE ON AVON

The majority of my racing this year (1976) has been in the inaugural Avon Roadrunner Production series, ten rounds in all at seven different circuits, from Carnaby in Yorkshire to Lydden in Kent. Machine used is a '75 registered Thruxton, but built from parts to early spec, ie: GP carb, BTH magneto, large bore pipe. The engine was originally destined for the Velocette Metisse, but got hijacked into the Thruxton for running in, and never reached its original destination. The Seymour-prepared engine was fitted with parallel roller main bearings, coil valve springs and rocker return springs, otherwise pretty standard, but well put together. The silencer is built from standard parts, but they are not necessarily in the same order that Veloce put them in! A Velo silencer has a loose baffle, where the flutes ran in the opposite direction to the fixed baffle. If you cut the flutes off, turn it around and re-weld, the exhaust gases have a freer run to atmosphere. It made it a tad noisier, but didn't seem to cause offence. Even with such a 'liberated' exhaust, it would not run cleanly on high revs on full throttle, if you rolled it off a tad, it picked up. But in the heat of a race, it is difficult to remember to roll it back a bit, with a host of Japanese buzz bombs in close quarter. What I would have given for a few hours on a dyno!

Cycle parts are standard Thruxton, as are gearbox and clutch, internal linkage for the box has been changed for the nylon jointed type supplied by Geoff Dodkin, to eliminate slop. The Avon rules only allow original equipment fairings, so mine was the only machine on the grid that year with a full fairing, which must have added a few mph to the top speed.

The first two championship rounds were at Snetterton, a very fast circuit which I did not think would have suited the Velo, but I got sixth and eighth places in the class. In the first race, I was scrapping with Eunice Evans who was riding her 500 Honda 4 and managed to get past a few times on the corners, much to her disgust, but she had the speed (and somewhat lighter weight) down the straight. With the usual lousy start, it was most satisfying to be able to pass groups of 500/400 Honda, and Yamaha down the straights.

I had to change jetting from standard to 350 main jet, but was still getting a bit of pinking when held flat out. Possibly the motor was a bit too 'sharp' for use with a silencer (it was meant to run on a mega).

Scrambler fork springs were fitted after the first round to stop it dragging on the floor, having nearly worn through the exhaust pipe in one meeting.

The next round was at Aintree, and I came 10th this time. It looked like people were getting the Yoshimura performance bits in the 400 fours, as some got away down the straight, and the corners were so smooth everything seemed to handle well there, so could not pull them back. The grass at Aintree may look like a lawn, but I was warned to stay off it. One Honda rider got it wrong, hit the grass, wobbled and fell off; it looked more like a ploughed field!

The next race meeting was on the Island again, the National event on the Jurby Road Course. The clutch objected to being run dry/wet alternately, and gave up in the last practice session, so I missed the first race fitting a replacement. For the second race, I was last away but through to 14th at the end of the third lap, lapping at 85, when the race was stopped to get the ambulance to an injured rider. This was the first time the Thruxton had been used on a megaphone, the rev counter was reading 6600 on 20 tooth down the mile-long Ballavarran straight. 400 main jet used with mega, 350 used with 'silencer.'

CADWELL PARK, AVON ROUND ON THE LONG GRAND PRIX CIRCUIT
It was my first and only time out on the long circuit, and it was much harder on my brakes than the Club circuit. You go through the flick-flick, over the Mountain, through Hall Bends and suddenly the Hairpin appears; Coppice is much tighter when you approach it flat out, as opposed to accelerating up to it from the Club Hairpin. I should have had a fifth place here, but the clutch was bedding in and started to slip on the last lap, so I was done by a 400 Yam going up the Mountain. I don't know where they take those photos of British Super bikes doing wheelies, all I could do was to slightly decompress the fork springs, and even then I was sitting on the back of the dual seat!

The first of the Brands rounds came next, and I was ninth in the class, in the midst of a whole line of snaking, wobbling 500s. From my view, six inches behind an overbored 380 Suzuki, now 475cc (and later, allegedly 550cc!), I don't know how the rider was staying on. He assured me he had the same feeling at times! The Suzuki was a bit of a 'mobile chicane,' snaking away. Down to Graham Hill Bend, I put the Velo where he wanted to put his Suzuki, which held him up enough for a few of us to get away.

I missed the next Avon round at Carnaby, but it sounded like a good one to miss. The circuit is on an airfield, with the course being marked by cones. Apparently the locals had developed a habit of sneaking inside the cones, and flipping them into the track of following competitors. It's a pity they couldn't fill them with concrete, then any competitors with broken toes could have been excluded for course cutting!

It was back to Brands again for the Avon, with two Velos out this time – Nick Payton riding his as well. We had to present our machines to the scrutineers at different times, as they varied (slightly) in specification. I got my best result so far, fifth in the class, with Nick just behind in sixth place. Two low placings in the open production races were followed by a four-stroke race, where we both fitted megaphones. There were bad starts for both, but we got with it after that, I finished third behind a Manx Norton and Brands Hatch specialist on a 250 Ducati, both Brands regulars, and Nick finished fifth. The difference that a mega can make was very noticeable here: 61 seconds was the best time on a silencer, but it dropped to 59 seconds with the mega, and two corners that I can take nearly flat out on the silencer, had to knock it off a bit on the mega.

The Cadwell short circuit came next, with both Nick and myself out there. I got sixth place in the Avon race, and Nick came 10th, so both of us were still in the points. A few incidents stand out at this meeting, first a 350 Yam caught the grass on the inside of the first left hander just before the hairpin, this threw the rider and bike across the track right in front of the main bunch, both travelling at about head height! Secondly, I had been trying to do a 500 Kawasaki all through the race, and decided to make a big effort on the last corner, diving inside at Mansfield and leaving braking very late. I just managed it, and the fellow was quite surprised, even more so as Nick was stuck behind me, the Kwacker rider got relegated two places in the space of six feet.

I went across to see the Manx after this event, returning the next Saturday for the Vincent Owners High Speed Trial meeting. There were many more Velos here, and they took a fair share of the awards. Nick Payton took two 1st class awards, also a second and third place. I should have had two third places, but on the last lap, I must have dozed off, because I found I had gone straight on at Park Corner instead of turning right. I ended up with a 1st class award, and second and fourth places in the races.

Wellesbourne, another airfield circuit, was the next venue for the Avon. In practice, I was passed by Pete 'PK' Davies, on Roger Slater's Laverda Jota; it gave a twitch (one of many I believe) and suddenly PK was doing a handstand, and I could see the track between his legs. As he hit the saddle, he hit the throttle, the rear tyre squealed and he was gone. I saw him in the paddock and remarked, "That looked exciting!" "More exciting from where I was sitting," was his reply.

The main hazard on that day was punctures from the stalls; the venue was also used for a country market, and quite a number of people picked up punctures, one fellow had two in successive races. The 500 class of the Avon that year was dominated by a scruffy RD 350 Yamaha, ridden by an equally scruffy looking rider – Phil 'Mez' Mellor. He normally won our class by a country mile, but his luck was out at Wellesbourne, retiring with a puncture. Another worthy competitor was Eunice Evans, riding a 500 Honda that she and husband Hugh had prepared. I was working for Hugh at Aitchee Engineering on Biggin Hill at the time. In production trim, wearing 'silencers,' Eunice's Honda had the edge on my Thruxton, but, with the mega fitted on the Velo, it was possible to match Eunice's speed. This was my best ride in the Avon series, third place in the class, 10 points, plus £4 prize money, professional at last! Nick Payton was also riding, he came fourth in class, also in the money.

The next race was an open Prod race, this time a clutch start, so I got off with the pack, and had a race-long dice with Nick, who beat me by half a length at the finish, despite going sideways out of the hairpin once or twice.

Last race of the day was a 500 four-stroke, we were both kitted out with megas again, and Eunice Evans was also out on the Honda. I thought it might be possible to beat her. In fact we were together for the whole of the race, in fourth/fifth positions just behind Terry Brook on another very quick Velo. I guessed I could squeeze through on the left-hander leading to the finish, and gave it the beans, but for the first time, it slid out from underneath me. I had visions of Velo and Honda rolling down the track, but Eun was just that little bit ahead and thankfully I missed her.

Sitting in the middle of the track, every one missed me, but I was in a slight predicament. My antique £25 leathers had burst their time-expired stitching upon impact and I was sitting there surrounded by acres of disconnected leather. I got a lift back in the ambulance to the first aid post, and the initial quick check appeared to show no damage, but subsequently found a dislocated shoulder, torn ligaments and muscles, and perforated eardrum, I was strapped up for six months and that was the end of my racing for the year.

We took the remains of the leathers to the chap Dad knew who repaired Lewis Leathers suits. He held them up, looked at me and said: "They don't fit well do they?" "Well enough for £25" was my reply. He agreed it was mighty leather so he measured me and I went back a few weeks later, he had completely taken them apart, and I had a set of (almost) fitted leathers. Alongside was a pile of leather which he had removed, which I left with him for patching other suits. Before his attention, the bum used to stick out by a foot, and I always had to tape or elastic the ankles otherwise they rode up over my knees. I still have them at home, wonder how they would fit me now?

After this meeting I was lying sixth in the Avon 500cc series, Hugh Evans took the Velo for a run in the last round at Lydden, but I was passed on points by a 400 Yam, so finished seventh with 37 points, which represented £37 bonus money from Avon for using their tyres. Here cometh the advert. The Roadrunner tyres suited the Velo very well, one advantage they have over the TT 100 is the very low wear factor, 29 races and plenty of road work, yet they still look good for another season. Also (on a Velo) you cannot get over to the very edge of the tread like the Dunlop, you wear the frame away first. I used 4.10 tyres on the rear, and 3.60 on the front.

In the few years I raced, I can remember very few times I failed to finish. I fell off at Cadwell twice (I must remember to let the brake off at the hairpin before cranking in!) Another time, I managed to deck my knee round Charlie's while chasing a pair of Triumph Daytonas, so I took it easier on the next lap, and suddenly, there was that grass-sky-grass-sky moment. I stopped rolling with a strange buzzing noise in my ears, the right clip-on had broken off and was under the saddle, the engine was revving its nuts off. I got over to it and lifted off the plug lead. I don't know how many volts went up my arm that day, but I must have flicked that plug lead into the next county, we couldn't find it. The valve collar breaking on the Viper at Cadwell was a rare mechanical ailment, and the last-lap spill at Wellesbourne when chasing Eunice Evans.

I only achieved one lap at the Killinchy 150 in 1977. We went over (Ken Law and Adrian Pirson were my ex-Dorking Velo club team) for the race, which was to be held over the Ulster Grand Prix course. When we went out for supper that evening, most of the pubs had window glass replaced by boards, but we found one with a few panes left in, so felt safe in there. As we sat waiting for supper, we were asked straight out, what were we doing there? Our different accents had given the game away, but having found we were from the Island (stop overs, not locals), and there for the Killinchy races, the atmosphere changed and all was well with the world.

That evening, sleeping in the paddock, or trying to, anyway, with the sound of the army half-tracks passing and helicopters overhead, we all felt a little uneasy.

In the race, going down Deer's Leap on the second lap, it felt like I had punctured. Pulling up at Cochranstown, I found that the swinging arm was loose, I had not properly located the off-set spacer that tensioned the chain on the Metisse. We left the bike over there and flew back, because there was no boat service until the next weekend. My toolbox caused great amusement going through security!

To qualify for the Manx, you had to have ridden at four or five circuits in those days to get a National licence. In 1977 a group of Manxies had decided to go to Snetterton to get the required signature. I remember following a Manx Norton up the start-finish straight in practice, when it suddenly slowed, twitched and then fell over. It was local man Dick Aldous, and the gearbox had seized on him. I polled a front row start, so heaved away and hit the saddle. The engine was running, but I was not going anywhere. The engine shaft shock absorber nut had failed, the spring had shot across the road, and that was the end of my race.

Another meeting at Mallory Park, with the usual furniture van full of Manxies and machines. This was the sweeping pre-chicane Mallory, and in practice I managed to hook a neutral going into the Esses, I swept right round

(continues page 113)

Competing

Bluehills Mine, the final section of the Land's End Trial, riding the MAF-framed MAC Velo. The Dowty forks had springs inserted: I wasn't prepared to trust the seals over that sort of terrain!

Not the most suitable trials machine! The Concord Couriers R80 RT, with the firm's insignia blanked out, at Millstone Edge, near Hathersage, Derbyshire. I even cleaned the section, road tyres and all!

VMCC trial. Behind the
bike is Keith Skillicorn,
Pat's former son-in-law.

At Hungry Hill on Bob Thomas' Douglas. Talmag Trial. (Courtesy Nick Nicholls)

Knackered! At the finish of the first Classic Manx Two Day Trial, on Bob Thomas' Light 500 Douglas.

If it wasn't the Steam Packet hat, it was the Loaghtan Wool hat I wore in trials. On the MAC at an unremembered location.

Dave Molyneux and Karl Ellison pose on the Dixon banking sidecar after the 1993 Sidecar TT. We had brought the bike over from Beaulieu to celebrate its winning the first Sidecar TT in 1923.

The 1922 Vauxhall four-cylinder. You don't often get to ride such an exotic machine – but I did!

Hillclimbing in darkest Devon. Riding the Viper at the Wiscombe Hillclimb.

The Manxcette, a Jim Lee-framed Thruxton. Gordon Gurney is helping me to position it for photographing at Guthrie's Memorial.

Trying to wear out the exhaust pipe on the Viper, at my first race meeting. Lydden Hill, Triumph Owners High Speed Trial meeting, 1971.

A group of Velo Fellows at Lydden Hill. Left to right: 'short-portly,' Jim Elliott, Norman Broadbridge, Bryan Clark and Ian Fray.

Roy Peplow heads off to start the 1965 International Six Days Trial, where he won a Gold medal. Fitted with road tyres, I made my racing debut on it at the Triumph Owners Lydden meeting.

Prewar racing at Cadwell Park – it looks like Mansfield, but can't be sure!

Sidecar action at a prewar Cadwell Park meeting.

Check out the crowds at the first road race meeting on UK soil after WWII, Cadwell Park, 1946.

Nick Payton, at the Cadwell Park 1000km race, 1975. I was co-rider with Nick that day.

'My' Velo Metisse, coincidentally wearing a number 1 plate, ridden by Anthony Woollon in the 1971 Senior Manx Grand Prix.

Cadwell Park High-Speed Trial action. Nick Payton leads a trio of Velos out the hairpin, I am taking a wide line and Pete Walters is sneaking up on the inside.

Dad holds the throttle and hands me the helmet. Brands Hatch, 1976; an Avon Production series round.

Brands Hatch Avon Production series action. I was scrapping with Des Foot on his Ducati, and we were probably carving up an orange-coated newcomer on the Yamaha.

'Short-portly' at Church Bends in my final race, the 1988 Classic TT, held that year on the Billown Course. I returned the bike with a destroyed engine!

Practice shot for the 1980 Manx, using the helmet the Scruts banned.

'Short-portly' leaving Parliament Square, Ramsey in the 1978 Newcomers' Manx Grand Prix.

Even my considerable weight could not keep the rear wheel on the deck on Bray Hill in the 1978 Senior Manx Grand Prix. An early race shot as the rear wheel rim is not full of oil!

The push-start of my Manx Grand Prix career. No 2 was Steve Winn (Matchless). The green-suited scrutineer behind is Norman Lamont – the other one!

Joey Dunlop (Yamaha) at the Southern 100, before he went through the gate behind me at Ballanorris.

PROVISIONAL RESULTS.   WEDNESDAY 6TH SEPTEMBER, 1978.

NEWCOMERS RACES.

PSN.	NO.	COMPETITOR.	HOME TOWN	MACHINE	TIME AND SPEED	

500 cc RACE

PSN.	NO.	COMPETITOR.	HOME TOWN	MACHINE	TIME	SPEED
1st	26	David Ashton	Chapel-em-le-Frith	492 Suzuki	125.35.0	81.25
2nd	8	John Davies	Burton-on-Trent	352 Maxton Yamaha	125.28.0	79.46
3rd	28	Davy Gordon	Portglenone. N.I.	498 Spartan	126.56.6	78.11
4th	10	Mal Marsden	Dalton-in-Furness	460 Honda	127.11.8	77.88
5th	19	Philip Odlin	Louth	492 Honda	127.47	77.36
6th	9	Kenny Harmer	Wigan	400 RD Yamaha	129.14.4	76.10
7th	20	John Minchell	Shrewsbury	398 Yamaha	129.42.4	75.70
8th	5	David Greenwood	Berkhamstead	351 Yamaha	130.17	75.22
9th	2	Stephen Winn	Hull	496 Seeley Matchless	132.21.4	73.53
10th	21	Norman Kneen	Onchan, I.O.M.	400 Yamaha	132.22	73.52
11th	4	Ray Corbett	Walsall	384 Yamaha	132.51.6	73.13
12th	1	Bill Snelling	Laxey, I.O.M.	500 Velocette	133.17.0	72.80
13th	25	Chris Harris	Newport, Gwent.	500 Cowes Matchless	134.38	71.76
14th	27	Barrie Baxter	Liverpool	460 Honda	134.57.4	71.52
15th	7	David Montgomery	Preston	351 M'd'ws Aerm'i	138.03.6	69.25
16th	6	Tom Krueger	Maidenhead	398 Yamaha	140.16.0	67.73
17th	30	Stephen Potts	R.A.F. Cranwell	352 Yamaha	149.03.8	61.80
18th	11	Dave Roberts	Hartlepool	492 Honda	153.07.2	59.68
19th	12	Steve O'Brien	Cwmbran	351 Cowles Yamaha	154.54.0	59.10

2 LAP FINISHER

	24	Stan Beck	Leyland	500 Bill Head Honda	1.15.09.0	6

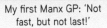

My first Manx GP: 'Not
fast, but not last!'

I am fairly certain that here I am
about to be lapped by Gordon
Pantall: it's not that I was
actually leading him!

My 1980 MGP mount, as bought and raced on the Jurby Road circuit.

Parliament Square shot of yours truly in the 1980 Senior Manx Grand Prix. The TZ fairing had to be raised around the Ducati lump.

In the 1980 Senior Manx Grand Prix, wearing the changed helmet that fooled my friends on the first lap.

A paddock shot during practice for the 1980 Senior Manx Grand Prix.

Receiving my finisher's medal for the 1978 Newcomers Manx from Deemster Luft.

Wellesbourne Production race action (silencer fitted).

Billy Guthrie on the Suzuki that he threw up the road in front of me when I was flag marshal at Hillberry.

The Triumph 3HW that I later used for MCC events and one ACU National Rally. Note the comfortable blow-up seat cushion!

The Manx trio at Warrington, rehydrating before the start of the 2012 National Rally: Chris Wallis, Gary Knight and myself.

Recording the Isle of Man for posterity

One of the early TT photo exhibitions we held at the Hodgson Loom Gallery, Laxey Woollen Mills.

Daydreaming: trying Bob Kewley's Greeves Silverstone for size in our TT exhibition at the Laxey Woollen Mills.

The presentation of the Hislop coins to his partner's family at the Steve Hislop statue, overlooking Douglas Bay in Onchan. The large facsimile of the coins were signed by many TT riders and auctioned off for charity.

Heinz Luthringhauser and Hermann Hahn (BMW) fly Ballaugh Bridge in the 1974 750 Sidecar TT. This was the 'lop-sided' engine machine, a 500 with a 252 barrel on one side to bring it within 750 rules.

Nigel Rollason (Yamaha) winning the 1971 Senior Manx Grand Prix.

Nigel Rollason and Donny Williams (Barton Phoenix) winning the 1986 Sidecar TT B.

the outside on the kerb, but held it. During one race, on the first lap there was the queue approaching the hairpin; in the track, rolled up as if it has come out of a box, was a chain. Round the corner was the chain's owner, frantically hooking what he hoped was first gear!

In 1977, the year of the Avon series, I rode the Thruxton to the Island, to race at the pre-TT meeting on the Jurby South road circuit on the Saturday before TT week. It was clocked at 120+ mph on the Ballavarran Straight. I had also planned to ride back across to Cadwell Park for the Avon round on the Bank Holiday Monday, returning to Manxland to finish my holiday. I met up at Jurby with Mick and Barbara Coombes, regular Vintage racers and MCC trial riders, who were also going to race at Cadwell, I hitched a ride with them to Lincolnshire, competed at my favourite track, then rode back to the Island to complete my TT holiday.

MANX GRAND PRIX

It seemed natural that, if you lived in the Island and raced bikes, sooner or later you rode the Manx Grand Prix. There were new races in 1978 for newcomers, so I entered the Senior Newcomers and the Senior Manx on my Seymour Thruxton Velocette Metisse, one of eight that were built by Ralph Seymour's of Thame. One of Ralph's riders, Fred Walton, lived on the Island, so I sought his advice about learning the course. I was living in Castletown at the time, and working for Bernie Lund at Grand Prix Motorcycles of Ramsey, so it was half-a-lap in the morning from Quarter Bridge, then the other half-a-lap in the evening. The best bit of advice Fred gave me was: "Never peel off too soon." By going deeper into corners such as Sarah's Cottage and the top and bottom of Barregarrow, the corner opened up to a curve. It works for so many corners around here. When the programme came out, I found myself as number 1 for the Newcomers, and 100 in the Senior.

To make sure I had learnt the course thoroughly, I used to ride a lap at about 2am – on pilot light. I had a 250 MZ Supa Five at the time (on Brit tyres: I was convinced I would leave the originals on until they wore out, that promise to myself lasted for about two weeks!) and would cruise it at night at about 65-70ish. With no lights coming the other way, you could abuse the white line and get a racing line sorted out. I wouldn't try that these days, so many drivers leave their lights off until well after dusk. I believe Joey Dunlop also put night-time laps to good use.

The first practice came; I set off okay, remembering I could use all the road. My course learning seemed to have worked, and I passed a few other Newcomers with white jackets on. I settled in for the second lap and, going along Cronk y Voddy, I felt something flick my bum, probably a stone I thought. Carrying on, the rear suspension seemed to have stiffened up. I thought no more about it until I pulled in, and tried to get off the bike, something was holding me in place. The smack on the butt was the collets of a rear suspension unit that had snapped off at the top, leaving one unit which was then fully compressed. The spring from the broken unit has wound its way through my leathers, hence why I could not dismount! And, I managed that second lap inside a qualifying time.

On the last practice session, I came round the Creg and gave it some beans, it was a beautiful motor. I took it to 6200, gave it a bit more and suddenly saw 7000 on the clock, it was like a turbine and was pulling like a train. I grabbed second, 7000, third, same revs and hit top, seeing 6600 just before Brandish (the old, original tight Brandish Corner). I mentioned this to Vern Wallis, Seymour's right-hand man, and got a severe rollicking for taking it to those revs. The engine was Seymour tuned, and fitted with parallel roller mains, rocker return springs and Fath valve springs. We computed it to be 132mph approaching Brandish, not bad for a sludge pump with a large entity on board. I never used those revs in the race (but I wish I had). They are now averaging, per lap, faster than my top speed down from the Creg that day.

Practice went off without a hitch, the bike was scrutineered at Mylchreest Motors, and the bikes were left there overnight. In the morning we rode from Westmoreland Road, along Peel Road and up Bray Hill to the start.

We started in pairs, my starting partner was Stephen Winn (Seeley). The flag dropped, we pushed off and after what seems an eternity I hit the saddle and it fired, before Stephen, if they had stopped that race then, I would have won. I was first on the road until just before Ballacraine, when I was passed by two Yamahas, who I re-passed through the Glen Helen section. They passed again on the Cronk y Voddy, but I was still fourth on the road at Ballaugh Bridge. I was always thrown across the road at Schoolhouse Corner, I probably went in 10th, and came out 20th, I must have been holding a whole load up. It was extremely misty across the top of the Mountain on that first lap, I was not prepared to take chances so was riding with the visor up. Coming down from the 32nd Milestone to Windy Corner, I was aware of a machine in front; couldn't see it, couldn't hear it, but I was getting two-stroke oil essence through the nostrils. I caught sight of the tail end of the machine that was issuing the fumes, and, knowing we were nowhere near Windy, I passed it. I glanced at the number; bear in mind this was the first lap. I was number 1, he was number 26! he had made up 2 minutes and ten seconds already on that first lap. I was the only man that day to pass Dave Ashton, who went on to win the Senior Newcomers class. As the mist disappeared, so did Dave. He graciously came into my TT photo exhibition a few years ago and acknowledged that, he was searching for Windy Corner when I passed him.

The Metisse petrol tank was quite bulbous, and so was my belly (more so in those days), which meant that down the Sulby Straight, with head tucked well down, the backside was well off the seat. It was a case of braking and burping in unison at Sulby Bridge!

It was an uneventful race, the lap speeds were very low, but there were no accidents or incidents in the mist. I finished 12th out of 20 finishers, at an average of just over 72mph.

Windy Corner, which is the nearest corner to Laxey where I live, also played a part in the 1980 Senior MGP – read on.

Just minutes after I finished, I was (willingly) coerced into joining the Manx Grand Prix Riders Association; about the only exclusive club that would have me as a member.

The Senior race went off without a hitch. Rounding Sarah's Cottage slowly, to waved yellow flags, resting against the hedge, with the front wheel alongside the engine, was a sister bike to mine, ridden by Manx man Peter Kermode. Peter was laid out in the road, but no one was touching him – what would you have thought? I was well distracted for a while after that. Luckily, he suffered no serious injuries, just knocked out, and the marshals were waiting for the chopper to ferry Peter to Nobles. My only issue in that race was that the engine was breathing a bit heavy; when I came in for the pit stop, the rear rim was full of oil. There was a catch tank for the breather, but we had exceeded its capacity. Nick Payton was mechanic that day, and he emptied the catch tank and the rear wheel rim. I received the chequered flag after five laps, but was still credited as a finisher, to claim a second finisher's medal from the Manx Grand Prix 1978.

Looking back now, I wonder whether I may have been quicker with a standard frame Velo than with the Metisse, it was a superbly built machine, but I had so many years riding/racing a standard Velo, the Metisse always felt different: you know how a Norton compares to a Velo, both super handling bikes. The Metisse would hold its line, then suddenly slide, mainly at Signpost Corner, whereas the normal Velo frame, although flexing (sit behind a Velo at speed and see the top suspension ears move), would give me more confidence. That's my view anyway. I would have kept the Fontana front brake, though.

Watching the Southern 100 in 1979, I was standing at Ballanorris Farm when Joey Dunlop came through the gate behind me! The steering damper had jammed; Joey slid off, picked himself up, accepted a fag and stood by the wall watching. As his bike tumbled across the field, it was shedding bits at every revolution. Tank, fairing, exhausts: you followed the line of Yamaha droppings and there was rest of the bike. The corner has been renamed Joey's Gate.

I rode the Southern 100 a few times. In one 1000cc race, I was approaching Cross Four Ways when I became aware of a bike alongside; a quick glance revealed his front wheel was locked, I could see the spokes. By now I was thinking of turning right, but it was still there, still locked! I was in a similar predicament: I was now on full lock, with the wheel locked! I made a very wide turn, just dabbing once, when Ian Bell, Marty Ames and Joey Dunlop sped away dicing for the lead. If I had cranked in when I wanted to, there might have been an expensive clattering of three 700 Yamahas and a Velo!

THE 1980 MANX

I decided to have a second bash at the Manx in 1980. The Douglas Motorcycle Centre had good contacts with Sports Motorcycles of Manchester; in its 'good but tatty' shed, Sports Motorcycles had a Ducati which had been part-exchanged by a guy who worked on oil rigs. He'd bought a new machine, ridden it for a few months, then gone back to work, earning a considerable bag of gold for his efforts; he fancied a change of bike, and that is how the Ducati came my way for £1000. It was a standard long-wheelbase electric-start GTE model. I rode it, as bought, at the Jurby West Andreas Club meeting. It was slower than the Velo, but was a comfortable ride. After that outing, I set to with a large cardboard box, into which went lights, starter motor, air cleaner and many other assorted not-wanted-on-voyage bits. That box weighed a ton, but so did the 'lightened' bike. A pair of pattern Conti-type silencers and larger carbs were fitted, with a Rita ignition system and a large alloy petrol tank almost completed the bike. A Yamaha 750-pattern TZ fairing wrapped round the bike, but it needed raising by a few inches. We retained the kickstart; this proved useful during the race, as you will find out later.

Chris 'Skid' Rowe fashioned the rear sets, and I was ready for practice. We had an on-off switch for the electrics to work, or not in this case! It was giving problems right from the start, during a practice lap the engine stopped halfway round the Gooseneck, but I was still making forward motion. A friendly marshal, Steve Parker, had hopped off the bank and was pushing me up the hill! Another time it conked out at Milntown. A spectator cycled home, found some wire and pliers, and effected a remedy by squeezing the switch terminals together. We ditched the switch in favour of a large spade connector on the battery after that.

That year, I had drawn number 116, the last man away, so I have seen the Manx Grand Prix from both ends of the field, having started at No 1 in the '78 Newcomers. Although in top speed, the Ducati was a lot slower than the Velo, I was able to lap faster because the five-speed box and larger capacity meant it would pull me up the Mountain. The Velo was hampered with just a four-speed box, with a big gap between second and third. It would rev out in second, but wouldn't get on the mega in third up from the Gooseneck until just after Guthrie's, no doubt hampered by a 'short-portly' sitting astride it.

At the weigh-in, my helmet was rejected; the outer layer had a chip in it (Jurby possibly!), so I had to get the all-red one for the race. Most of my mates missed me on the first lap, they were looking for the striped helmet. The helmet lining settled during the race, where it was nice and firm to start with, but it dropped forward when braking for Governors and the like, I had to keep pushing it back on the last two laps.

Back to the 1980 Senior Manx. It was an uneventful ride. The pit stop went well, Velo club friend Brian Henn refuelled in short order, but I was prevented from kick-starting so Brian had to leg me down pit lane. I normally dropped a gear for the 32nd, dropping a further gear for Windy. One particular lap, I went round 32nd in top, when I dropped into what I thought was third, it felt like I had missed a gear. Braking in a straight line, I took to the grass and ended up adjacent to the stone wall, in an upright position. Finding neutral, I booted the bike into life and was away again almost before the marshals had moved. As I pitched it into the two left-handers of 33rd Milestone, I thought 'mud on tyres,' I expected to be flagged off after five laps, but there was no sign of a flag so I carried on, being convinced the roads open car was on my tail. I saw no other rider from the start of that lap right round to the Graham Memorial (Bungalow Bridge). It was a strange feeling; most of the spectators were making their way home, so when I got to Sulby Bridge on that last lap, instead of a wall of spectators there was just a policeman and marshal!

'Not Fast But Not Last' was my motto, so I figured I could be around fifth or sixth from the bottom of the list. In the prize presentation, they always started from the bottom up. A lot of names were called out, but not me! It transpired I finished 45th out of 66 finishers; because I was tail-end-Charlie on the road, my time had been quicker than 21 others that had finished. Three MGP rides, three finishes.

In 2008, as a guest of honour of the Manx Motorcycle Club, I was accorded the honour of flagging off No 1 (Ivan Lintin) on the 30th anniversary of my ride.

In 2018, I was again invited by the MMCC to flag off the first starter of the Newcomers Race. This was not so easy, as I was wheelchair bound, without a left hip in place; the Ramsey Cottage Hospital had kindly given me permission to be absent for a few hours. Norman Cowin got me into place next to starter Kevin Brookes; the day before their guest starter had flagged the first man away, then dropped the flag! I was under strict orders to keep hold of it, then quickly pass it to Kevin to flag the rest of the field away. I performed the start, first man away was Mike Browne (Kawasaki).

I was interviewed by Nick Jefferies for MGP TV, I looked like Quasimodo in the chair, because I had forgotten to take a cushion to keep me more upright in the wheelchair! A brilliant day, meeting lots of friends and ex-racers, visiting the Manx Grand Prix Supporters Club marquee and the 38th Milestone (TT and MGP Riders Association), a wonderful fillip after nine weeks in hospital.

THE 1988 CLASSIC TT

I thought the 1980 Manx would have been my last race, but I was chatting to Steve Woodward around the time the Classic TT on the Southern 100 course was mooted for 1988, he mentioned he had a 500 Norton, and would I like to ride it? Too right! The machine had seen service for many years in Vintage Club events on the 'adjacent Island.' It was a very standard Model 50 push rod model, even to the cast iron flywheels, and a fibreglass tank and mega made it look a proper racer. In the race, I was involved in a dice with American Benni Rodil (BSA). One lap, braking for Castletown Bridge, I thought the brakes were working very well, until I lifted the clutch, it was a piston seizure that was retarding progress! It was still running, and I knew we were only a lap from the finish, so coaxed it round that last lap. At almost the exact spot it had nipped on the previous lap, the piston completely folded up, and I free-wheeled round the corner. It is not that far to push, but it was quite a slope up from Castletown Corner before the gentle slope to the finish. Ron Kitching was waiting for me to pass the flag, his arm was aching by time I got there! There were bits of piston to be seen in the mega. That, then, was my final race, and the leathers were hung up for the last time.

FLAGGING AT HILLBERRY

In 1981, I was flag marshal at Hillberry, for the TT. Thursday afternoon practice had started, and Irishman Billy Guthrie led the field on the first lap. As he cranked into the corner, he caught his footrest on the kerb, and slid up the road. I looked back towards Brandish; the road was thick with riders hoping for a fast lap. Frantically flagging away, I was pleased to see that both Billy, unhurt, and Suzuki had parked themselves on the pavement by the Glen Dhoo campsite. Later that session, Bill Smith cruised down with a fuel-less RG500. Hearing of Billy's plight, he wandered up the road and came back with Billy's tank, he fitted it to his RG500 and carried on practising; I wonder if he reimbursed Billy?

THE ACU NATIONAL RALLY

I rode the ACU National three times, on three very differing machines.

1986: First up, a Moto Guzzi V50 II, a great run, in good weather. During the night, I came across a huddle of bikers, working on another V50, it was my old MCC trials riding pals, the Met Police team. The ignition switch had packed up, not an unusual occurrence with these machines. They were fixing it by taking all the wires from the switch, squeezing them together with a mole grip, which they insulated by sticking it into a large mitt; they got to the finish! We continually passed each other, going in opposing directions, as on this Rally you set your own route. My first National Gold.

1987: I was on the 1941 3HW ex-WD Triumph, rigid and girders. A pair of pals from the Wimbledon Club had always wanted to ride it, so I sorted a route and we rode together. Riding to Wantage on the M4, my start location, the petrol pipe came loose on the carb, and I ran out of petrol, this on the hottest day of the year. I was knackered when I got to Mick Coombes' bike business in Wantage, I was revived with tea and Dextrosol tablets! The old 3HW was not a fast beastie, but we kept pounding on through night, the day broke and we got to a check point, at which point my riding partners begged me to let them have a break! They lay down on the concrete forecourt of a garage and were soon fast asleep. I gave them a good half hour's kip before rousing them and getting back into the Rally, we gained Gold that day too. The sprung saddle on the rigid Triumph worked well, but I had the added assistance of the front half of an Abasport inflatable seat cushion. The second and final Gold.

For the National, you are given a set of controls with varying mileage between them, you have to plan a route which takes in as many checks as possible in exactly 400 miles.

2012: In 2012, now living on the Island, a few of the Manx Saturday Club started to think about riding the National Rally. My two-wheel transport at that time was a 400 Suzuki Burgman scoot, my companions that day were Gary Knight (Suzuki VL 1500 Intruder) and Chris Wallis (BMW). We sorted out a route, no sat nav for us, I just looked it up on Google Street View. We got the Saturday morning boat to Liverpool and waited for the 2pm start at Warrington. We headed west, through to Doncaster, and going down the M1 we met a monsoon of a downpour; with screen and leg shields, I escaped the worst, but my riding mates had to endure being damp for many hours until they dried out. We pressed on, but Gary was a little out of sorts that day, and had to take frequent breaks. Down the A1, one check was at the former Wait for the Wagon pub, by the Black Cat roundabout where the A428 from Bedford meets the A1. My sister, Tricia, lived just a quarter mile from there, so we headed there to give Gary a break, he went to bed for an hour, feeling much better after that. We then headed for Stevenage, and then Ongar. With Google Street View, I had viewed and memorised quite a bit of the route. We pounded on, over the M11, and found the checkpoint in a scout hut at Ongar. When we stopped there, Chris turned and said to me "How did we get here, you never looked at any maps!" It was all those years of long-distance trials and despatching that helped! We spent some time in the Harrow area, finding the check. I whistled round a sharp corner, then heard the sound of a stove being dragged across cobbles; the footboards on Gary's beast were decking, Chris got showered by the sparks! We carried on into London; despite living down that way for years, I had never been to the Ace Café until that day, probably spent too much time there chatting to Mark Wilsmore, then headed west into Oxfordshire. Passing Brize Norton Aerodrome, Gary gave the Suzuki, with its 'liberated' pipes, a few beans, which started up all the car alarms.

I love night riding, at dawn, the blacks turn to dark green and suddenly the countryside colours burst into life. We got to within a couple of checks to the finish, but ran out of time, they were closed. We set sail for the Ravens Café, Prees Heath, the final control, where we got our finishers' awards, a hearty breakfast and then headed for the Sunday evening boat home, I don't recall much of the boat trip!

Recording the Isle of Man for posterity

MANX MUSEUM

Nowadays, I assist the Manx Museum (Manx National Heritage), and we are currently working on a TT/MGP database, trying to get it as correct as possible. There are other databases out there, but to my mind they are seriously flawed. For many years, the passengers were never even mentioned in the official ACU TT results books, and by initials only in the 1970s. I have managed to find many Christian names, but still missing quite a few. I get occasional TT queries sent to me from the Museum Library or through Facebook.

I have worked on other Museum projects, too: the Manx section of the crew list of fishing boats (CLIP) around the UK was one, also helping catalogue a huge collection of glass slides from the Second World War.

Manx Museum Assistant Keeper Matthew Richardson has written a couple of books about the TT (*Dave Molyneux*, *TT Titans*), and I have assisted him on these in a private capacity.

EXHIBITIONS AND THE MGP SUPPORTERS CLUB

Just a few weeks before TT 2008, I was chatting to John Wood, owner of the Laxey Woollen Mills, whilst he was clearing the upper loom room. "I reckon I could put on a photo exhibition here," I suggested. "Okay!" said John. I have the facility to print A3 from home, so that was the size of the photographs. The first year, I used regular glossy lamination for the prints, but with the big windows in the gallery, it wasn't easy to see them. This was rectified for the second year by using museum-quality matt lamination. For the first few years I had to source boards to display the pictures on. As time went on John did a lot of work on the gallery, aided by Julia Ashby Smyth, who is curator for the many arts and crafts exhibitions held in the gallery through the year – I just hijacked it for two weeks for TT and MGP! The exhibition is on an upper floor of the Mill, the Hodgson Loom Art Gallery, named after a 1914 loom that still sits in the room: John still weaves the Manx tartan and other cloth, and it is a working Mill. Because its Arts and Crafts exhibitions have proved very popular, our little two-week exhibition now intrudes on the Mill's calendar, so we mutually agreed to change venues. From 2020, our exhibition moved to the Ballacregga Corn Mill, near the Laxey Wheel.

During our first exhibition a Scottish chap came in, spending quite a long time looking at the photographs, and said, "Lovely exhibition, pity there is not a Steve Hislop pic." This was Jim Oliver, who gave Steve his first race on the T B Oliver Yamaha. I said: "Come back tomorrow." That night, I found a photograph of Steve and hung it the exhibition the next day. From that day until he passed away, Jim always came to the exhibition, there will always be a Hizzy picture each year, together with a Mike the Bike and Bob Mac portrait.

Jim Oliver was a great supporter of the races, and bringing on young talent. His company, Olivers, celebrated its 100th anniversary in 2019, it was formerly a millwright before getting into transport.

I enjoy watching the visitors to our exhibitions, as complete strangers get chatting about their favourite hobby. The stairs put some people off, though; due to his advancing age, World Champion co-rider Stan Dibben no longer calls in, but we still correspond through Facebook.

One elderly chap came in, with multi-coloured hair (his daughter was a hairdresser, she always sent him to the TT in flamboyant colours). We instantly hit it off. Rick Howard was very into vintage and especially veteran machines. He very often sent a package of early photos over to use in the exhibition. One year, we were upstairs, eating the Craftea Weaver's excellent cakes and quaffing coffee. "See you later," he said as he left. Sadly it was not to be; riding back to his campsite, he felt unwell, parked the bike, got off, sat down, laid down and passed away that evening in Noble's Hospital. Ain't life cruel.

I have met thousands of people who come to the exhibition every year: riders, mechanics, and fans from all over the world. Some of the stories I hear form part of the following year's exhibition, a few others cannot be repeated. I would love to know who the rider was, who had a few too many scoops the night before the last practice, but needed another lap to qualify for a 1950s Manx. His missus got into his leathers and rode that final qualifying lap. Another time, a well-known rider said to a mate, "Who was riding your bike last night?" "I was," came the answer, to which my friend said: "It wasn't, the guy who was riding it when I passed him had hair!"

I was told the story of Heinz Luthringhauser's 'lop-sided' BMW. The TT rules specified you could not ride a 500cc outfit in the 750/1000cc sidecar race. Heinz had goosed his big outfit in practice in 1974. To qualify to start, and get his start money, he grafted a 254cc barrel on one side of his 500. He set off, expecting to pull in early. The bike was going well, so he pressed on and finished second. The scrutineers have to measure the first three; they took the barrel of the '500' side of his engine and were set to exclude him, but he got them to take the other cylinder off, and the swept capacity was greater than 500, so the result stood.

Amongst the regular visitors to the exhibition was Nigel Rollason, who won on two wheels (1971 Senior Manx Grand Prix), three wheels (1986 Sidecar B on the Barton Phoenix) and no wheels, when he sailed the Round the Island yacht race. A different trio to Freddie Dixon who won on two, three and four wheels in the 1930s. Nigel was in when an Aussie film crew came along, who were following one of their local sidecar crews, and were delighted to chat with a real sidecar ace. Nigel sadly passed away in early 2019.

In 2014 we had a visit from a group of old Saltbox friends – Saltboxisti? Among them was my good MCC riding companion Del Whitton. Sadly Alzheimers had claimed Del; there was no recognition from someone who I had spent hours chasing round the lanes of the Kent countryside and the hundreds of miles on MMC events. Ain't life cruel.

Winner of the Manx Two Day Trial, the Manx Grand Prix and a TT, Nick Jefferies very often stays just down the road to the exhibition, if he spots a bloomer, he quietly lets me know. I take the photo off the wall, reprint it with the correct information, laminate it and rehang the next day.

There is no entrance fee to the exhibition, but we rattle the Green Bucket in aid of the MGP Supporters Club Welfare Fund.

The MGP Supporters Club started when Mick Bird fell off at Quarry Bends in practice for the 1975 MGP. Although not seriously injured, it took the ambulance a while to get to him. That evening, a group of marshals were gathered in the Raven Inn, at Ballaugh. "What we need is a helicopter for the Manx practice," someone said. Gwen Crellin stood up said, "This is the first meeting of the Manx Grand Prix Helicopter Fund." Amongst the founders was Raymond Caley, who ran the little shop at the Sulby Crossroads. The helicopter was paid for by the Government for MGP race week only, and for many years the MGPSC raised the money to provide the practice-week chopper, passing it to the Manx Motorcycle Cub.

Recently, the TT organisers have become involved in the Festival of Motorcycling, so they now fully fund the chopper. The MGPSC now concentrates on assisting riders and their families after incidents at the Manx. Gwen became famous as the 'Lady in White,' marshalling outside her house at Ballaugh. She became patron of the Club, and in 1984, she was awarded an MBE for her services. Her home was a magnet for riders any time of the year, if you retired from practice or race nearby, there was always a tableful of scoff to lessen the disappointment. Ago, Mick Grant and others used to stop and exchange pleasantries with Gwen on the Classic Parade Laps. At her funeral in Ballaugh Church, the vicar asked "Who has been kissed by Gwen?" Almost everyone there raised their hand!

During the winter, we set to collate a new set of photographs; the previous year's pictures are then passed to Rosie Christian, who runs the Sulby Glen Hotel, for exhibition in a marquee behind the pub. Rosie also supports the MGP Supporters Club, so she rattles the Green Bucket there too.

When the second race of the day was cancelled a few years ago due to the weather, the Radio TT anchorman at the time, Charlie Lambert, said on the radio, "Well you know where to go, Bill's exhibition at Laxey." That day the room bulged to saturation, I have never had so many people in, I had a couple of TT and Manx winners, plus a Radio One DJ and his dog in that day. Andy Kershaw was at that time living on the Island; a real biking enthusiast, before living here he used to come for the TT with fellow DJ John Peel.

I have no leaning to one particular style of music, I just like what comes to my ear and sticks. I guess I am drawn to anthemic sort of music; the 1812 Overture, Mussorgsky's Pictures at an Exhibition through to Fanfare for the Common Man, Red and Gold (Fairport Convention). I first heard the Tchaikosky's 1812 Overture at Bible Class in Mitcham (along with Les Gray, who was lead singer with the band Mud). I am guessing a lot of my likes mimic the tempo of single cylinder bikes, mainly Velos.

We have seen the Scottish Taiko drummer group Mugenkyo at the Villa Marina twice, they make you want to get a bike out and blast a lap! As did *On Any Sunday* when we used to go to the Midnight Matinee at the cinema in Strand Street.

PHOTOGRAPHS

For many years now I have bought or been custodian of many thousands of photographs of the TT, MGP, Southern 100 and Andreas Racing, from their inception to date, plus some Ulster Grand Prix and selected UK short-circuit meetings (1950-1959) under the title FoTTofinders Bikesport Photo Archives. I now co-own the Island Photographics collection, which forms a major part of FoTTofinders. After cataloguing this collection, and before taking control of them, someone 'lifted' a number of files, mainly with an Irish connection. We have a fair idea who this individual was, but cannot confirm it: the gent concerned has 'pleasured her majesty' more than once due to his nefarious activities. Our marketing arm is currently TTracepics.com, an English-based company that provides not just photographs, but mugs, mouse mats and jigsaw puzzles (surprisingly popular). We currently have around 20,000 images on offer, but will increase this number over the years. TTracepics markets our products worldwide, via eBay and Amazon. The 'Smokin' Bantam, Harvey Williams leaping Ballaugh Bridge with a cigarette on during practce for the 1952 TT, is one of our best-selling prints, in all formats.

In 1978, I went looking for pictures of my MGP rides, S R Keig's had over 200 sheets of films, but uncollated and catalogued, like most of their postwar photos. I offered to do this work for a fee, dependent on sales. Around this time, I was chatting to Steve Colvin, who has been filming the races since the middle '70s, so I started working on his collection too. I knew that Island Photographics had a selection from postwar to 2004. The photographic firm was started by Bill Salmond, was sold through various bodies and ended up renamed as Island Photographics, run by Monica and Ian Clark. As expected, the early postwar pictures are limited by the cameras, but the collection really started to blossom in the mid-'50s. Because Bill was the sole photographer at that time, he was limited as to his locations, plus the need to get the films back to his shop and develop them to have them on display in his shop in Strand Street that evening. The best of the photographs will eventually appear on TTracepics.com but most will need a little cleaning and touching up before offering for sale. Digital is so much easier to manage, just annotate and bang them in!

The Keig Collection has since been sold to a German collector.

Quite often I get passed packets of photographs with no information on: this is quite a challenge, especially if it's 1950s MGP shots, no fairings and with most of the riders wearing silver Cromwell lids! If I can identify just one rider on that film, I can then chase what year he rode that number, practice shots are difficult from those days, as there were no side numbers. You have to check background colours to see if the film is race or practice.

Another one of my hobbies is to assist the Manx Philatelic and Coin Bureau with pictures and text for stamps and coins. J Graham Oates and Bill Lockington Marshall featured on a stamp in 1993.

I was asked to provide comments for a coin pack depicting Mike Hailwood that was launched in 2018, I wrote a piece as a fan of Mike, and they printed it in full on the Limited Edition set.

In 2019, I again assisted the Post Office with text for the limited edition Steve Hislop coin set, celebrating Hizzy's first ever 120mph lap, in the 1989 Formula One TT.

Our photos have also been used for the Bonham's auction catalogues, a quite superbly produced publication. I was passed a shoebox full of photographs taken by Gordon Schofield, mainly from Cadwell Park, some from the first ever race meeting to be held on UK soil after WWII, Good Friday and Easter Monday 1946. There were alleged to be around 15,000 packed around this Lincolnshire circuit for that first meeting. They were packed 20 deep to see the restart of racing postwar. Winners that weekend included Maurice Cann (Moto Guzzi), Tommy Wood (Junior Velocette), George Brown (Vincent HRD), Eric Oliver (Sidecar Norton) and Jack Surtees, John's father.

PICTURES AND EXHIBITS

Honda GB's Neil Tuxworth contacted me, as one of his TT guests of honour a few years ago was Aika San, former head Honda mechanic for Hailwood and many other stars. He wondered whether we had any photos of Aika, and it just so happened we have quite a few. The whole Honda entourage came round to our little wooden bungalow in Laxey, and left clutching a USB stick of memories for Aika.

We were contacted by Peter Haynes regarding using some of our photos as references for his paintings. He had never previously exhibited in any manner, but I persuaded him to bring some of his artwork to display in our exhibition. His work is fabulous, my favourites are Mike Hailwood on the naked Benelli at Braddan Bridge in the 1962 Lightweight TT, and Bob McIntyre on Bray Hill in the 1952 Senior Manx on a 7R, he finished second on it after winning the Junior that same year.

We also exhibited John Hancox's work; he has a classic eye for the period bikes, Hancox Art, worth looking up.

A loose and infected hip problem stopped me from attending the 2018 11th running of my exhibition, but it is now an annual part of the TT entertainment, as, for the first few years, we were the only photo exhibition during the fortnight. Due to health issues I decided to abandon our 12th TT: to get the pics sorted and printed in my current lame condition was too much. J J Ribbons and the Ballacregga Corn Mills used my pictures as placemats during TT 2019, and my pictures also graced the wall of the Ramsey Swimming Pool Café.

The ex-Murrays Motorcycle Museum at the Bungalow is due to open as a café in either 2020 or 2021, and we hope they will feature our work there. It's always flippin' cold up there on the side of Snaefell, I hope they have Bungalow Broth on the menu!

BONNEVILLE

Manxies have featured well out at Bonneville. In 2012 Laxey rider Richard Barks (father of actress Samantha Barks) was the first person to clock a 200mph run on a semi-faired 500 Yamaha on the salt. The machine was a Yamaha Thundercat fitted with a 400 crankshaft to get the capacity right. When they arrived at the Salt Flats, they raised the Manx flag, which was mistaken for a Nazi swastika! At the end of that successful week, they were crowned 'Rookies of the Year,' it took people many years to accomplish what they did first time out. There have been four Manxies who have ridden the Bonneville Salt Flats, and every one has returned with a record. We displayed Richard's machine in one of our exhibitions: it took a bit of lifting up the stairs to the gallery! On another occasion, when we had the loan of a Gilera 4 GP machine, we enlisted the help of the local fire brigade to get it up there. Another Bonneville record-breaker we featured was Ralfy Mitchell's 250 turbocharged Royal Enfield, the first ever Enfield to break a speed record at Bonneville. Two race-prepared engines went 'pop' in the first week there: they had thrown a standard power unit in the crate to use as spares, so Richard Birch set to, stripped and detailed the engine to run with the turbocharger. On the very last day of Bonneville week 2016, Ralfy upped the supercharged 250cc record, which had stood for many years, by 5mph. Ralfy is also a whisky connoiseur, and has many YouTube videos (search for ralfydotcom), where he reviews and critiques the amber nectar. Alcohol does not play a big part in our lives, however (unlike a lot of inhabitants of this rock in the Irish Sea). We like a slug of Irish Meadow whisky liqueur at infrequent intervals, but can't remember when we last bought a bottle.

WRITING AND PUBLISHING

For a long time I had been hearing stories about a Manx motorcyclist called

J Graham Oates, who rode an Ariel outfit trans-Canada in 1928, and again in 1932. There was also a James Walter Oates who built the Aurora, the only Manx-constructed motorcycle. I say constructed, as all parts were bought in and assembled on the Island. Very quickly I found they were one and the same person. I made contact with Graham's sister, with the intention of writing an article about his exploits. She was the custodian of a large number of his scrap books, photo albums and diaries, so I started writing my first book: *Aurora to Ariel, the motorcycle exploits of J Graham Oates, a pioneering Manx motorcyclist.* Whilst I was researching and writing the book, I was visited by Graham Oates Jnr, his son. Asking me where I got my references from, I pointed to a shelf and said, "These books." He had never seen them; when Graham swapped wives during the war, David had stayed with his mother. He is now the rightful custodian of all the Oates books, diaries etc.

The book was published in 1993, and the first edition sold out. In the meantime I had received more details of the British Empire Motor Club, which Graham helped form in Canada in 1928, so in 2010 I published an expanded second edition, which also subsequently sold out, and it is now only available as a Kindle ebook. All this would have never taken place if a dustbin lid had been in place: Gladys, Graham's sister, was visiting his second wife Betty while she was preparing to move from Moose Lodge into Ramsey. As Gladys passed the dustbin, she looked in and found all the diaries, scrapbooks, etc, in the bin. Betty had not been a fan of motorcycling, and used to chase people off who came to see Graham about his motorcycling days, even old friends from Canada.

In 2009 Graham Oates was inducted into the Canadian Motorcycle Hall of Fame.

One of the Vintage Club's founders, Titch Allen, had written the history of Veloce Ltd, which was serialised in *Motorcycle Sport*. Titch, together with Cyril Ayton, editor of *'Sport*, and myself, decided to publish the book, containing Titch's writings, complemented by further photos. We published 2000 copies, which sold out, followed by a further 1000 copies.

I was instrumental in getting Peel resident and Vincent fan David Wright into authorship; he has since written many books on the Vincent HRD marque and the TT, his first five books came out under my Amulree Publications imprint; I am pleased to say they all sold out of their print runs, and *Travelling Marshals* went into a second, enlarged edition. One book, *Vincent & HRD Motorcycles – How They Were Promoted and Sold*, had only 998 copies printed, one per cc.

I have co-written and published many books since I wrote *Aurora*. Among them were *The History of the Manx Grand Prix 1923-1998*, and *Honda the TT Winning Years*, both written in conjunction with 'The Voice of the TT' Peter Kneale.

The History of the Clubman TT Races was co-written with Manx competitor Fred Pidcock. Fred had been in contact with us for pictures of his 1976 Senior

Manx GP ride (he rode a Suzuki twin). We were discussing our mutual interest in the Clubman TT, and I suggested, "Why don't you write the book?". "Never done anything like that," said Fred, so I asked him to write a provisional chapter, which I showed to David Wright. David agreed with me that Fred's effort was worthy of publication, so I sorted out pictures and results of every race and every race lap from the Clubman races.

In all I published around 21 books, and wrote or co-wrote many more for UK publishers. Our photo archives have been widely used in publications, sometimes without our knowledge!

I provide the Manx Motorcycle Club results book, which now is available as a pdf file to download from the internet.

The TT, a Photographic History with foreword by John McGuinness, was published by a UK company, and ran as second-best seller in the sports section on Amazon for quite a few weeks after it was published in 2015.

TT REVISITED

With such a collection of pictures to hand, I was persuaded to make a series of videos for YouTube, entitled 'TT Revisited.' I already have 1947, '57, '67, '77 on-line, with plans to make many more, when I get 'aroundtoit'!

FILMS

During the winter months, I occasionally give film shows at the Peveril Club's MCC headquarters at the Knock Froy Scrambles Track, near Santon. Over the years, I have amassed about 200 motorcycling films. Mostly they are copies of copies, so the quality is not 'mint' as a certain rider might say. But the content overrules the quality; I have a film of the 1923 TT, which includes the very first Sidecar TT, won by Freddie Dixon/Walter Denny, plus Tom Sheard winning the Senior TT, also on a Douglas. The Sheard family still own his machine and the Banking Sidecar is on display at Milntown House, near Ramsey. With info gathered from the Manx Museum Library archives and Mortons Motorcycle Media, I intend to add a commentary to this silent film.

These films have also proved popular during our exhibitions; one year Ferri Brouwer, ex-Yamaha and Arai helmets was in, later that year he sent me copies of some of Yamaha's racing films to add to the collection. A favourite film is of Bill and Maggie Tuer climbing the Klausenrennen in Switzerland aboard their Morgan. They attack the hill in style, setting the fastest time of the day, faster than solos. It looks a fabulous road, I would love to ride it, but not at the speed they use!

The BSA Gold Star Owners' club held their annual rally here one Manx Grand Prix. Courtesy of Colin Washbourne, who worked at Small Heath for many years, I was able to give a show of films featuring mainly Small Heath machinery in racing, trials and scrambles, plus a look inside the factory.

CLASSIC TT MAGIC AND THE RUSSIAN SKY CREW
In 1996 I was asked by Greenlight Television to help it make the video Classic
TT Magic. That year, Moto Guzzi had sent over two of its fabulous V-8s for the
Parade Lap, one to be ridden by Bill Lomas, the other a replica, built and ridden
by Giuseppe Todero, whose father, Umberto, was one of the development team
on the V-8 with Giulio Carcarno, and he just happened to have a full set of
drawings. If you have enough Euros, you could be the owner of one of these,
like Sammy Miller!

Double world champion for the Mandello concern (1955 & 1956 350cc), Bill
Lomas was not the rider of the V-8 in the 1957 Senior TT – that was Dickie
Dale – but Bill had ridden it to take world speed records, and also in GPs.
His machine was fitted with onboard cameras. Sadly, Giuseppe slid off his at
Braddan Bridge, but the only damage was a dented fairing, and his pride!

As well as the TT Classic Lap of Honour and the Classic TT, we featured
some of the one-make club rallies in the film: the Velo one at Niarbyl was a
natural, and we also followed the Vintage Club events.

A few years later, I was asked by the TT organisers if I would conduct a Russian
Sky film team around to film all aspects of the TT meeting. The producer spoke
a little English, but his cameraman none! Despite this handicap, I took them
to many places, from Bushy's TT tent, through the racing and Vintage club
events, and finally a sidecar Trial held on Cunningham's Camp. They were
fascinated by the Groudle Glen Railway across the valley from the camp, but
more so by the sidecars; they had never seen the like. I think it made for good
viewing in Russia.

new books • ebooks • apps • newsletter • special offers • gift vouchers
www.veloce.co.uk / www.velocebooks.com

Recording the Isle of Man for posterity

(continued)

A frequent visitor to our TT photo exhibitions, Yorkshire's Nick Jefferies (Honda) winning the 1993 Formula One TT.

Gwen Crellin MBE presents the contribution cheque from the MGP Supporters' Club to Manx MCC's chairman Jack Wood at the 1980 Manx Grand Prix prizegiving.

The Smokin' Bantam! A classic (and best-selling) shot from our FoT Tofinders collection, Harvey Williams flies his BSA over Ballaugh Bridge in practice for the 1952 Ultra Lightweight TT.

Ray Pickrell winning the 1971 Production TT on 'Slippery Sam,' wearing Percy Tait's helmet.

The IoM post office coin set commemorating Mike Hailwood.

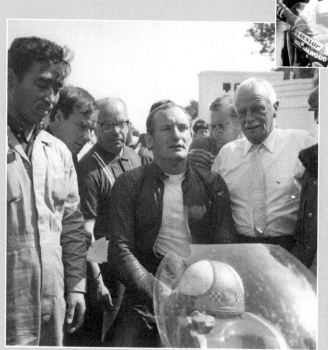

Mike and Stan Hailwood with Honda's chief mechanic Aika San, celebrating Mike's 10th TT win, equalling Stanley Woods' total.

Peter Haynes' superb painting of Mike Hailwood on the Benelli in the 1962 Lightweight TT, the fairing was ripped off at a pit stop.

Peter Haynes with another of his paintings of Eric Oliver and Stan Dibben in the Ulster Grand Prix, 1953.

The first Manxman to hold a Bonneville record. Richard Barks went over 200mph on an part-faired 500 at his first attempt on Bonneville, 2012.

The only Royal Enfield to hold a record at Bonneville. Ralfy Mitchell with his supercharged Crusader on the salt flats, 2016.

The British Empire Motor Club badge. The club was formed by Graham Oates in the late 1920s.

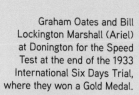

Graham Oates and Bill Lockington Marshall (Ariel) at Donington for the Speed Test at the end of the 1933 International Six Days Trial, where they won a Gold Medal.

Graham Oates during his winning ride in the 24-hour race held around the Halton Hills, Ontario, 1928.

Graham Oates relaxes after winning the 24-hour race around the Halton Hills.

The launch of the Manx postal stamp featuring Graham Oates. Left to right, David Cretney, MHK (member of Manx Parliament) Bill Lockington Marshall (Graham's 1933 passenger), David Oates (Graham's son) and yours truly. Square 4 loaned by Paul Hipkin.

Running repairs to the sidecar wheel. Nearing the end of his trans-Canada trip, Graham Oates resorted to any measures to get to English Bay, Vancouver.

Graham poses with the Aurora, the only Manx-built motorcycle.

David Wright, author of many books about Vincent HRD, on his Comet.

Co-author of *The History of the Clubman TT* Fred Pidcock (Seeley Suzuki, Parliament Square, 1976 Senior Manx Grand Prix).

'The Voice of the TT' Peter Kneale commentating from the TT Grandstand.
(Courtesy Isle of Man Newspapers)

Bill Lomas rides the Guzzi V8 in the 1996 TT Parade Lap.

Travels abroad and closer to home

Mancunian born but living in Canada, Harold Cosgrove (Maico) in the 1973 Ultra Lightweight TT.

My only two-wheel sojourn on Canadian soil. Al Johnson (right) and myself at the venue for the start of the 24-hour event at Halton Hills that was won by J Graham Oates (Ariel) on his trans-Canada epic in 1928.

Mike (now Michelle) Duff, Arter Matchless, 1963 TT.

Michelle Duff rides a replica four-cylinder 250 Yamaha in the 2007 TT Parade Lap.

Graham Oates' Ariel combination on the Kettle Rapid Bridge, en route to Churchill, Hudson Bay, 1932. The outfit was ridden on the railway lines for thousands of miles …

… but the bobbins didn't always keep the outfit on the rails! Graham Oates had to wait until the next train came along for assistance to get back on the tracks. Getting near Churchill, Hudson Bay, 1932.

A section of Canadian rail, as seen from the driver's cabin en route to Churchill in 2000.

Proof. The bottle of water Graham Oates collected when he arrived at Churchill in 1932.

WITHIN 200 MILES OF
ARCTIC CIRCLE
AND FURTHER NORTH
THAN ANY RUBBERTYRED
VEHICLE
HUDSON BAY
CANADA
Oct 3 RD 1932

We were well insulated (and highly coloured) against the Hudson Bay cold, whereas the locals were quite used to the weather up there!

A close encounter of the furry kind! This bear and her cub were hanging on to the side of the observation platform at Hudson Bay, Canada.

Left to right: Harold Cosgrove, yours truly, and Chris Carter, taking part in a Daytona chat show in 2000.

Geoff Blanthorn and Ed Gilkison at the Gilkison ranch, Lake Bay, Seattle.

The Velo spares department in the roof of the boat shed at Ed Gilkison's, Lake Bay, Seattle.

MCC trial riding partner Geoff Blanthorn, making my trials MAC look like a moped under him!

A scrambler Velo shares a huge garage with some inferior makes at Ed Gilkison's place, Lake Bay, Seattle. The Velo appears to have left its calling card!

Fame! Quite a small township, but it bears the family name, Snelling, California.

King Ludwig II's Neuschwanstein Castle, near Fussen, Bavaria, Germany, visited on our way to Italy. It was a hike to get to, but well worth it.

Dreaming: astride a Guzzi V8 in Giuseppi Todero's workshop just outside Mandello del Lario.

The Museum at the Guzzi factory, Mandello del Lario.

A magnificent V-twin Moto Guzzi we spotted in a private museum in Italy.

Part of the Manx contingent at Bisley. Short-portly in red jacket, Frank Coffey, and Cliff Prosser.

The missus, shooting for the Island at the Commonwealth Shooting Federation (European Division) meeting at Melbourne.

Just Bluffing! The southernmost point in New Zealand. By gum it was blowy, we were hanging on to the post as well as ourselves!

The victorious Croydon & District team with the magnificent City of London trophy, 1984. Left to right: Austin Wiltshire, the short bearded one, Ken Parr, Gerald McCartney and John Twyford.

The missus and a group of medal winners from Marown school at the Manx Guild music festival.

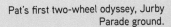

Pat's first two-wheel odyssey, Jurby Parade ground.

On the Brooklands Banking in 2016.

Got the missus a job as a labourer! Taken during a trip round the construction site of the Eden Project in Cornwall.

Otis and Mark at play, Spinney Road, Chawston.

Travels abroad and closer to home

TRAVELS ABROAD

CANADA AND AMERICA

The day Pat and I met in 1994, she talked about going to Canada, as she had a sister living in Stratford, Ontario. Stratford is a town of around 85,000 population (about the same as the Isle of Man), the River Avon runs through the town and it has a couple of theatres which hold Shakespeare's plays. Every year in the spring they release 24 white swans into Lake Victoria, which are accompanied from their winter quarters to the river by the Stratford Police Pipe Band, a wonderful sight. Our first trip over there was 1999, and we have visited Canada many times since. It is a wonderful country, and the people are so friendly and obliging. We sought out some of our TT friends over there, and popped down to Niagara Falls on that first trip to visit Harold and Mary Cosgrove. Formerly from Manchester, Harold rode the TT from 1962 to 1972 on a variety of machines, Itom, Honda, Kreidler, Yamaha and Maico. We had expected to stay just an hour down there, but the brand new hire car refused to start when we tried to leave, so we stayed the night and got to see the Falls and the other tourist attractions. There was a fabulous view of the Falls from one of the large hotels, you went up to the 14th floor and saw the spectacular view from the end of the corridor – but it has now been ruined because they built another big hotel in front of it. One year, we traversed the Freedom Bridge into America; it never gave us the comfortable feel of Canada, so we turned tail and went back to the comfortable country, but not before we bought our duty-free allowance. You were supposed to be out of country for three days with the duty free, but we acted like thick tourists and got away with it!

Another trip out was to meet with Allan Johnson, one of the head men of the Canadian Vintage Motorcycle Group, of which I think I am the only member from the Isle of Man chapter! We kitted up and Al took us to ride part of the route for the 24-hour run that Graham Oates rode (and won) in 1928 during his trans-Canada trip. Al has a wonderful collection of bikes, including a Levis and a big Brough. The Brough was alleged to be a police bike; when he stripped it out, the gasket behind the oil pump was made from a parking ticket – enough proof wouldn't you say!

Another Canuck TT friend who we stayed with in Canada was Michelle Duff, formerly Mike Duff, Yamaha works rider, three-times TT third places, and three GP wins to boot. Michelle lived about two hours north of Toronto, in what is known as 'Cottage Country,' an area of forests and lakes; most of the houses there are summer vacation accommodation. Michelle was one of the few to live out there full time. The road was called 'Nature Wild Road' and it lived up to its name well. From the car park off the main road, you had to traverse a piece of the Cambrian slate and then find Michelle's road. It was a switchback past lakes, and then you found yourself at her self-built wooden house. She had dogs, cats, the occasional visit from bears, and the raccoons used to scoot along the verandah to pinch the nuts from the bird feeders. It was idyllic, just where a nature lover needs to live. Michelle and I went out in her canoe, and we were halfway across the lake when her dog jumped off the bank and chased us. Pat was convinced he was going to drown, but he made that trip with his mistress most days. In winter they skied on the lake.

We were watching a Moto GP race at Michelle's one day, and the commentators were talking about tyres: soft, medium, or hard compounds. "In my day, they were black round things, the last place man had the same tyre on as Mike Hailwood!" said Michelle.

Michelle has now moved to Nova Scotia, she has been back to the Island a few times, once to ride the replica Yamaha four that cost the factory £250,000 in the TT Parade Lap. She is held in high esteem by the Hamamatsu factory bosses and the mechanics who worked with her. Michelle's biography *Make Haste, Slowly* is an excellent read, telling of a rider's climb from privateer to works rider.

In 2000, we went on the Via Rail from Toronto to Vancouver. On the way across, we stopped off at Winnipeg and rode the train to Churchill, on the shores of Hudson Bay, to retrace the trip Manxman Graham Oates had made in 1932. His Ariel outfit was rigged so as to ride the rails, with outriggers front and rear.

Via Rail knew the purpose of our journey, we were relaxing in the observation car when the co-driver came and spoke to us. He invited us up to the cab, where we stayed for a few hours and saw the same view that Graham had seen 62 years ago. The permafrost is thawing, so the train was travelling very slowly, but the view has hardly changed in those 70+ years. The rail trip to Churchill was suspended in May, 2017 after severe flooding damaged the track beds and bridges.

We also took back with us a bottle of water that Graham had collected when he got there. There is a small mention of him in the Churchill local library.

Whilst in Churchill we took a helicopter ride over the area, flying over 'Miss Piggy' a C-46 cargo plane that crashed on take-off in 1979; it still sits where it crashed, a tourist attraction (and rendezvous for local youths!). Coming in to land, I persuaded the chopper pilot to fly down the line of the railway, with the grain elevators in view which must have been a welcome sight for Graham Oates after travelling all those miles on the rails. We also saw the Northern

Lights – the Aurora Borealis, after which Graham Oates named his motorcycle – but as there was a Polar Bear alert in force that night, we didn't stay outside too long! (We have seen a better display of Northern Lights at home from just above Laxey. Manx Radio tells us if there is any activity due, so on one occasion we went to the north-facing aspect above Ballaragh, and saw the sky quarter filled with the rays and quarter filled with the curtain.)

We also went on a Tundra Buggy trip; whilst they were serving a snack, I was alone on the rear observation platform. A bear with cub at her side came up and stood on her hind legs against the buggy, she was that close I could have reached down and touched her, but I didn't dare. I was hoping that Pat would come out and video our encounter, but she was getting warm inside. The bear was that close, I could barely get my camera far enough back to focus. Our eyeballing interlude lasted over ten minutes, then she and the cub wandered off. An encounter I will never forget!

Polar bears are the main tourist attraction of the area, but not welcome in the town; if they transgress the town limits three times, they are then helicoptered away from the area.

In 2004 we flew into Hamilton Airport, where Harold and Mary Cosgrove met us and then drove us from Niagara to Daytona, for the Classic races. They have taken this 1100-mile trip on many occasions. At the first café we used in the States, Mary said "Find a meal you both like, order one portion and an extra plate" – it was plenty big enough. We traversed many states in America on our way down, saw some sights, even some snow which stopped the traffic in Virginia on the interstate highway: they only have one snow plough in that state. At motels we stayed in en route, we always sent the oldest one of us in to book, so we got seniors rates!

To drive through the tunnels into the Daytona circuit and see the bowl was awesome. At one point, a group of us formed in the paddock, a mixture of American, Canadian, German and Manx TT enthusiasts. It transpired that two of the group rode the same 1956 Senior Clubman race; David Hagen, from Oregon had finished 12th, Maurice Candy, solo and sidecar racer who emigrated later, was 16th, both on new Gold Stars they had purchased directly from Small Heath. They did not know each other until then.

Whilst in Daytona, Harold and I were invited onto Chris Carter's Daytona Radio show to talk about the Island and the TT.

The full Harley Davidson racing team was at Daytona, as well as US stars like Gary Nixon; the bikes were dwarfed by the size of the arena, but had the same feeling as a Classic meeting back home. We went to Key West whilst down there and also had some (close-ish) observations of alligators, or crocodiles, Florida is the only place they co-exist, through the Everglades. Whilst in Florida, we took the opportunity to visit America's space capital Cape Canaveral, marvelling at the size of those satellite launchers, and even managing to squeeze my fingers around a piece of moon rock from many thousands of miles away!

Whilst on one of our Canadian vacations, in 1999, we took a Royal Caribbean cruise from Vancouver to see the Hubbard Glacier. (This cruise was that year's venue for Harold Cosgrove's amateur video maker's conference.) The views of the glaciers are amazing especially when a large lump 'calfs' off and crashes into the sea, and we saw plenty of whales on this stage of the trip too.

I would recommend anyone to take just one cruise in their life, you wouldn't believe you are at sea when watching a girl juggling whilst riding a mono-cycle in the theatre. There was literally a shopping mall (or village) in the middle of the ship, and a casino. I changed five dollars (big spender) took two pulls and the machine spewed forth money, we were scooping it into cups and caps. I did no more than head back to the cashier's booth to change it back into notes and have never been in a casino since.

On our way back down south from the glaciers, I was talking to a couple from Florida who had never been that far north. "I would love to have seen the Aurora," said the chap. I had been keeping an eye on the sky and said "Keep looking north." Within a few minutes a full Aurora erupted across the sky, the beautiful curtain, then the rays. I think he thought I had switched it on!

I saw more bikes in Canada on Vancouver Island than anywhere else in the country. The Driftwood Motel, Sydney, where we stayed on the Island, with plenty of driftwood stacked up on the shore, could have been the setting for the Bates Motel in *Psycho*.

After returning from the cruise, we headed south to visit our friends Ed Gilkison and Geoff Blanthorn at Lake Bay, Washington State. We were given a hard time at the Border by American officials because we were carrying fruit. They went on for seemingly hours, until they turned the packet over to see 'Produce of USA' on the back.

For many years, most of the Velo spares from the USA have found their way to Lake Bay. Ed's family used to make fibreglass boats, those sheds are now full of Velo spares and bikes. I went into one loft, and it took me back to my Velo days at Geoff Dodkin's. There were many boxes with part numbers that I recognised, and Ed must have gathered the world's entire collection of MAC layshaft third gears, absolutely hundreds of them, he even had spares for LE and Valiant models, which were never imported to America. Whilst there Geoff took us to the Mount St Helen's visitor centre where we watched a time-lapse film of the mountain sliding away in May, 1980. Terrifying!

We visited some of Ed's friends down in Port Angeles; visiting what can only be described as a 'greasy spoon' sort of a café. In there I had the most fantastic clam chowder ever. Bill two-bellies scores again!

Geoff Blanthorn, one of my MCC trial riding partners now lives on the Gilkison Estate. When he lived adjacent to Crystal Palace football ground, he was for many years the editor of *Fishtail*, the magazine of the Velocette

Owners' club. Geoff also worked for the Transport Authority in the UK, he was a stickler for transport safety (despite the state of his own bikes!). If anyone from a commercial or bus company upset Geoff, he could easily and legitimately ban their vehicles from the roads. He now assists Ed in the workshop. Geoff and I rode many MCC trials together whilst living in the UK.

Ed and Geoff have both visited the Isle of Man for the TT. I woke up one morning to unexpectedly find them fast asleep in my living room, I didn't even hear them arrive.

I was shown a photograph of the California township of Snelling, on Highway 59, also there is a Fort Snelling in Minnesota, on the banks of the Mississipi – no connection with my family, but I'm still looking for my rich uncle with a garage-full of vintage bikes!

ITALY AND EUROPE

In 2001 we booked an Italian holiday, Pat, myself and Pat's friend Adrian Pilgrim, the former chief Hansard clerk to Tynwald, the Island's Parliament. Adrian and Pat shared a love of languages and music; Saturday night she went to his place in Baldrine, whilst I saw my biking buddies around Laxey. An avid linguist, Adrian wanted to appreciate the Romansch language at first hand; this was spoken in certain areas in Italy, Switzerland and Germany. On our way there, we visited Mad King Ludwig's Neuschwanstein Castle. A nearby town, Fussen, has three legs as their coat of arms.

We had no accomodation booked in Mandello del Lario, and spotted a sign saying 'Hotel Al Verde.' We followed these signs, past the Moto Guzzi factory, then through the town with its narrow streets climbing ever upwards, still following the signs. We finally came to a bar, with a very narrow entrance to a hotel signed behind it. Down a very steep (1 in 5) slope, there was the hotel. "This can't be the way in," Pat exclaimed. "Well we might be going in by the back door, but it's a bed for the night." So down the hill we went. "Yes" they had rooms – first floor, Room 5. As we turned to climb the stairs, the whole stairway was a collection of photographs of Moto Guzzi racers, this was where Moto Guzzi used to house its riders and guests!

On Tuesday evenings they close the restaurant to the public, it's open just for hotel guests and a group of friends. Most of these friends have Moto Guzzi connections. There are retired workers, one chap ran the engine build section (I blamed him for my V50 throwing a rod up the Kingston bypass!), road testers, even a senior manager when the factory was still owned by the Guzzi family. "Pity you aren't staying longer," said Mario de Marcellis, owner of Al Verde, "I could show you a better collection of machines than the factory have." I had taken some photos along with me, from the TT and Ulster GP, which were well received, and also showed a few films from the 1950s, Dutch TT and the 1957 Senior TT.

I had broken my denture chomping on a stunning mixed grill, so was reduced to mumbling a fair bit. We visited the Guzzi shop in Mandello, started by Dario Agostini (no relation to Giacomo), and run by his daughter at that time. She recognised my plight, and rang a customer of hers who just happened to be a dental technician, like Dad. He was waiting for us across Lake Como, and took us back to his place; the apartment had a beautiful view over the lake, and we chatted to his English partner. The smell of his technician's room took me back all those years to Dad's workshop. In half an hour it was repaired, reinforced and he refused to take anything for the work.

We also made our way to the Moto Guzzi factory. The Museum was a bit disappointing as it was only open for around an hour a day, though it housed splendid machines from all years, and a full-size bronze statue of Omobono Tenni, a favoured son of the Guzzi family.

The new Guzzi management did not seem too interested in the historical pictures of the marque, but did allow us round the yard to see the wind tunnel that Guzzi used to perfect their machines. In the 1950s they would spend days, tweaking fairings, seat and handlebars to get that extra mile an hour. Opposite the wind tunnel was a large dial, the number of bulbs that lit up measured their results. All the instrumentation had been taken out, but the straps were laying alongside the bike cradle as if they had just wheeled the last machine away. Although the mid-50's Norton possibly had the edge on top speed, the fuel efficiency of Guzzi meant they could hold back until the Nortons were forced to pit, then take over. The 1955 Ulster GP film shows this in glorious action.

On our second trip to Mandello and Al Verde, as soon as we booked in I asked Mario about visiting the private collection. Within a few days it was all arranged. This private Moto Guzzi collection is housed in a nearby town, I have not named it, as I am not sure if the collection is open to the public. I was invited there by our hosts from the hotel. We entered through electric gates, which closed behind us, and were escorted into a warehouse. This contained around 30 Airone and 30 Falcone models of varying years, absolutely sparkling, plus a few other models, including the half-track 'Mulo Meccanico' from WWII. The owner realised we knew the status of such machines, and we were invited into a second warehouse, which was stuffed full of racing machinery, including three V-8s, one original, two repro. There were a lot of Moto Guzzi's successful single-cylinder racers, pre- and postwar, and the very rare, three-cylinder, across-the-frame supercharged 500, called the 'widow maker,' which used to be raced on road events round the many lakes in that area of Italy. In one corner was Omobono Tenni's 1937 Lightweight TT-winning bike, still covered in Castrol R, as if it had just finished the race. I was there for just over an hour, I could have stayed all week! The place was equipped with sleeping accommodation, a shower and a bar.

AUSTRALIA AND NEW ZEALAND

In 2005 Pat represented the Island at the Commonwealth Shooting Federation in Melbourne. We combined this with a holiday in New Zealand; after shooting in Australia. We went across to hire a camper van and do the tourist route round the South Island of NZ, including a helicopter trip to land on the Franz Josef Glacier. On our way down to the ferry across to the south island, we stopped at the Te Papa museum in Wellington. Just outside the café they have a Britten V-twin, mounted in a wheelie position. It was interesting to see how many stopped to view it and comment that it was a true Kiwi creation; the film of John Britten and his machine is called *One Man's Dream*, but it was a crew of dedicated engineers who created this magnificent machine.

At Bluff, we ventured down to Stirling Point, the next point south from us was the Antarctic. It was a hellish windy day, so we held on tight to the signpost whilst our picture was taken by another couple, we then took one of them with their camera, got back in our respective cars and high-tailed back to the nearest café for a hot drink!

ADVENTURES AT HOME

SHOOTING

I took up rifle shooting in 1980 at the Peel range (which forms the cellars of an antiques shop these days). TT Marshals Frank and Mary Crellin introduced me to the sport, I went down, got fitted into a rifle and had about six shots. Later that evening, I was in the Peel team. I scored 72 on that first night, one has to start somewhere. I stayed with the Club, managing to get into final of the NSRA Eley Competition. I loaded my rifle and gear onto a coach from the Island (they wouldn't allow that now!), and was met at Euston Coach Station by Mum and Dad. After a night at home, we went to Bisley Camp, home of English shooting, where I finished third in my class, then back on the coach to the Island that night.

When I moved back to Mitcham, I joined the Croydon Rifle and Pistol Club, based in Beddington Lane. The range was a former London Transport war-time Home Guard range, and the backstop for the pistol butts was a double decker bus covered in sods. The range backed onto the Beddington Sewer Farm, and it was alive with animals. One night, after shooting and feeding on pizza, we were sitting around the table in the club room when someone muttered "Quiet!" A few seconds later a fox walked into the room, round all of us sitting there, then walked out again. Some may rate them vermin, but they are beautiful animals. It got so tame that Club Captain Reg Wilson used to buy dog food, he would put half a tin in a hub cap; she would come and take it away for her cubs, then come back for her dinner. One day, when we were shooting the 25 yards from inside a shed to the targets outdoors, we got a 'cease fire' call as the fox walked between ourselves and the targets.

We won our division of the City of London rifle league in 1984, and were invited to the final of the City of London Cup at County Hall, Westminster. We were in a high division, and it was normally accepted that a lower league team who shoot above their average would take the honours. Not that day: all five of us had a perfect day, and we were presented with the trophy by Deputy Greater Council Leader Illtyd Harrington (apparently Ken Livingstone did not like the rifle range). The trophy was magnificent, bigger than the FA Cup, and worth thousands. We took it back to Beddington Lane, photographed it and then returned it to the safety of County Hall.

One night someone came down to the range with a box of very old .22 rounds which they had found in a cellar when clearing their house. Not having a licence, they wanted the club to dispose of it. We chose the very oldest rattiest Webley single-shot pistol, and went out onto the range very late at night. Some rounds were marked up tracer, they provided a spectacular sight going down the range. Others did not ignite, those are called 'hangfire.' You had to keep the gun pointing down the range at all times, as some went off seconds after the trigger was pulled – very dodgy! Some never fired at all, these rounds were taken back to the armoury, dismantled and the powder burnt off.

I carried on rifle shooting, and added .22 pistol to my accomplishments. Croydon has a full complement of small-bore ranges, 25-yard, 50-metre, 100-yard and standard pistol. My 50-metre was not too hot, but I was better at the hundred yards. One day, I was shooting a set of Dewar league cards (2 x 50-metres and 2 x 100-yards). My 50-metre was crap as usual, so I settled on the 100-yard range, alongside Ken Parr, one of GB's top shots at that time (his son Ken Jnr is now a full GB international, but he wasn't even thought of in those days). I was shooting well that day, they were going where they should. Alongside, all I could hear were curses, only one of us was getting it right. Ken could not believe it when we retrieved our targets. They went away for scoring, I retrieved mine and still have them laminated at home, my only 2 x 100. I was lucky enough to win the Eleanor Trophy at Croydon, a day-long competition of rifle and pistol disciplines. Most of the competitions we took part in were postal, the targets were shot, witnessed and sent off to a central scoring committee, I was fortunate enough to win some individual and team medals whilst with the Croydon club, nice chunky things, compared to today's plastic trophies.

In addition to the Croydon Rifle and Pistol Club, I shot for the Pratt's team. Pratt's was a large department store, owned by the John Lewis group. Their shopping bags were emblazoned with the John Lewis logo – who wants to be seen walking around with a Pratt bag! We shot at an inter-John Lewis shop shoot in Nottingham in 1985. Pratt's had a very accomplished team, we won the individual, team and clay pigeon shoot that day. On the pigeon shoot command 'Start' we took all the targets down with our first shots, it took some teams nearly two minutes to get theirs down

When back on the Island, I briefly shot for the Castletown Diamonds, then with the Police team, and finally I pitched up at Laxey and District Club, which shoots in a former boathouse in the lower Laxey Glen.

When I first shot outdoors on the Island, the Sinclair Range was but a field, we pinned our targets to pallets and shot from a concrete pad open to the elements. These days, it is a National standard range, with electronic targets, and a wonderful club house with all facilities; the Island has produced many world-class shooters, Stewart Watterson, Harry Creevy and Rachel Glover amongst them.

PAT

When Pat came into my life about 25 years ago, she accompanied me down the Laxey range. She shot one card off a cushion, then asked how it was done properly, so we got her into a jacket, sling and away she went. She had enjoyed plinking at fairs, but had never shot seriously. She was a natural; although monocular-visioned due to cataracts, she could get all the 'polos' in line. In 2004 Pat and Suzanne Cubbon represented the Island in the C.S.F.E.D. (European division) finals, finishing in silver medal position behind the Welsh team and ahead of the England girls. In her short shooting career, which started after she got her pension, she was Ladies Island Rifle champion three times, at the time when her nearest challenger was Suzanne Cubbon, a fellow Laxey member who had won the title 15 times. One year, Pat also finished second overall, just one point behind Trevor Tubman, but she considers her finest shooting success to have been on the shoot in Australia, despite only finishing 12th. She was holding onto third place halfway through the competition, despite using 55 sighters, so time was of the essence. The wind changed direction, and caught her out for a few shots, which dropped her down the field, but still beating a lot of established shooters, this with a borrowed and heavier rifle than her own.

Pat was presented with the Sword of State by the Isle of Man Rifle Association; our only regret was that she was passed over to shoot in the Commonwealth Games, despite being the Ladies champion that year. I guess some thought her too old. Our shooting days are now over, but we retain happy memories, and the odd trophy.

People wonder why she is still known as Pat Burgess, even though she is Mrs Pat Snelling. For 53 years, she was a teacher, first in Stockport, then Canada and then St John's in the Island, finally becoming deputy head at Marown. So many staff, ex-pupils and families know her as Mrs Burgess, or Mrs B, I am more than happy for that to continue. She loves music and the Manx language, she put many entries into the Guild, the Island music festival, and released a tape called *Kiaull yn Aeglagh* (music of youth), featuring pupils from Marown School. Two of her pupils were accepted for Cheethams Music Academy in Manchester, Emma Christian and Bronwyn Williams. Recently, world-renowned soprano

Kate Dowman released a CD of Manx music called *Whispering Tides*, which features many songs that Pat taught her when she was around seven years of age. Kate acknowledges Pat's contribution to her musical prowess on the sleeve notes.

To this day, we meet people who Pat has taught from way back when, she has memories of them as little nippers, they are anything but that now!

Pat was never into bikes, but in 2016 she went to Road & Track Motorcycles and bought a 125 Yamaha scoot. To get her prepared for her test, I took it to the Parade Ground, on Jurby Camp, where she took her first faltering yards on two wheels. After very few weeks, she was confident enough to go to Matty Lund's Marine Drive centre, to prepare for part one of her CBT. He took her on a long run down the south of the Island, the first time she had ridden a bike on public roads, but passed with flying colours. She did not carry on with the second part of the test, our Staffy-Cross-Lab Otis means more to her than a bike licence, but she proved to herself she could do it.

Although Pat's aim maybe uber accurate, her sense of direction is anything but. We were touring America, and stayed the night at the Freestone Inn, possibly a play on words, as it was a timber-built hotel near Mazama, Washington. Well after midnight, I heard my name being called. It was pitch-black, and Pat had found the bathroom, but was unable to find her way out; she found the corridor, so guessed that was wrong, then back into the bathroom from where she was plaintively calling for help! My own sense of direction went haywire when in the southern hemisphere in New Zealand and Australia, it took a few days to work out things were 180 degrees from where they should be!

Most evenings after tea, I slide into the chaos I laughingly call the 'office' to sort pictures. Pat settles down to watch what she calls 'social history' but what I call classic *Coronation Street*: she was brought up in Stockport but has a Manx Grandfather who was a Laxey miner.

AND OTIS MAKES THREE!

Pat was never without a dog in her life, and a second husband wasn't going to change that! After a succession of Rottweilers, by 2012 she decided to get something smaller. We couldn't find a pet-friendly dog on the Island, so she browsed the net, finding a Staffy-cross Lab playing with a pair of Sphinx cats, at the West Yorkshire Rescue Group. We arranged to visit Huddersfield, where the group homes pets, rather than kennel them. When we got there, we sat down, Otis came in, and jumped on our laps – self selection!

For many years, our main transport was a smallish camper-van, small enough to travel on the Steam Packet as a car, but big enough to contain the three of us (Pat, Bill and Pooch) comfortably. We've travelled in everything from a Romahome, through Bedford CF to an Itaca, a Fiat Scudo-based van. On one occasion we went away to purchase one from the Midlands, and on the way back to the Island, we stopped for a break at an M6 service station. Hearing noises outside, I peered out of the curtain to see a car transporter being unloaded next to us. It was obvious what was afoot! I declined to make any rash move against that highly organised gang of car thieves, you don't get this old by being rash!

BEAMISH MUSEUM

Pat and I had seen the Beamish Museum featured on TV a lot, but wanted to experience it ourselves. A long trip across country to County Durham was well worth it: The Living Museum of the North lives up to its name (it won the Museum of the Year award, under the direction of Stephen Harrison, who also won the award for Manx National Heritage). There is plenty to see and do at this 300 acre site – you can hop on and off free buses, trams and carriages to get around. Although many things have changed, Pat could still relate to a lot of the social conditions depicted here. From there it was not that far to get to Antony Gormley's Angel of the North, and to see and touch this structure was awesome!

My luck was to take a life membership of Manx National Heritage an awfully long time ago, when it was affordable. The reciprocal arrangements with the National Trust means we can visit its sites for free; we try take in at least one site per visit; Styal Mill, not far out of Stockport is a favourite.

BROOKLANDS

In 2016, we were in southern England, so we popped into the Brooklands Museum. One of their volunteers, Andy Lambert, I had not seen since our last day at the Elliott School in Putney. Andy's business was heavy haulage, none heavier than the aircraft that he used to deliver to the Brooklands site. He is now one of Brooklands longest serving volunteers, so I had the best guided tour of the place ever. The race track opened the same year as the TT races started, 1907. Large sections of the huge speed bowl has been removed, but the Member's Banking and Test Hill are still in place. During WWII, Vickers placed a hangar right on the start-finish straight to dissuade any thoughts of racing. With lottery funding, this has now been re-located, so another piece of this historic venue can be used again. The motorcycle side of the Brooklands Museum is quite small, but with the motoring history, aviation history (including Barnes Wallis' bouncing bomb and other projects) and the London Transport Museum on site, it is worth a full day's visit. To stand on the Member's Banking is the equivalent of coming to the Island and standing on the startline: pure history.

TT VIEWPOINTS

I have viewed from a lot of areas around the course, a great many of which are now prohibited to the public due to Health and Safety. The Gooseneck is probably my favourite, you used to be able to sit road-side. In the '60s, you could hear the Honda 4s and 6s wailing their way along from Sulby, you lose the sound as they go behind Sky Hill, then hear them leave Ramsey Hairpin and burst round Waterworks.

One year in practice, I was joined on the Gooseneck bank by someone whose face I recognised, but couldn't place. It was the then Lieutenant Governor of the Island, Sir Laurence New. He had popped 'off-duty' to watch the races on his Honda. He was sent to King William's College for schooling in the '50s, and had been taken to watch the practices by Cannon Stenning, another great fan of the races. After his term of office as Lieutenant Governor was over, he had to leave the Island during the next term, but had already bought a house above Laxey, and came to live back here at the earliest opportunity. He and Lady New walk the length of Laxey Prom regularly.

Guthrie's offers quite a few viewing points, you could walk under the road and get to view from both sides. Parking can be an issue, with so many marshals required these days.

The Creg ny Baa is the nearest TT vantage point to home, it allows you plenty of space to roam. During one Manx practice, the first man through, Pete Beale, was aiming for a quick lap. Unfortunately, his lap ended outside the pub. He hit the barriers and went high in the air; as he was coming back down, I swear he was trying to kick the bike!

The end of the Cronk y Voddy tells you who has learnt the course; I was watching practice there one day when Steve Hislop went through full chat on a Honda RC30, a little while later a chap went down a gear, on a 125!

The bottom of Barregarrow also sorts out the handling, we were sitting on the hedge (now a prohibited area) when an evil-handling Laverda came round, snaking its way to Kirk Michael, running along the kerb calmed its antics, but did nothing for the blood pressure of us spectators!

It is always good to spectate at a point where they provide watering and de-watering facilities (especially at our age). Many church halls lining the course earn good money by providing snacks.

RELATIONS

My sister Tricia and her husband Cedric managed a 40-acre small holding on Chawston Moor, near the A1 by Bedford. Cedric's family, miners from Bridlington, were allocated the plot when the Northern Mines were closed, by the Land Settlement Association (LSA). Cedric was the first grower of celery for Marks & Spencer, and spent hours on his knees planting them in acres of greenhouses.

Since I have become a 'frequent flyer' to the Linda McCartney clinic at The Royal Liverpool Hospital, I have reconnected with my cousin Linda Lukehirst, my only Northern relative. She works at a Liverpool hospital, and accompanies me to appointments, as she understands their lingo (I know bikes, she knows bodies!).

OUR RETREAT
45 years ago, Pat's daughter wanted a horse, so Pat bought a two-and-a-half acre field. The horse never materialised, but she kept hold of the field all this time. We saw a TV programme about Agroforestry, and figured to use the field in this way. We attended a Martin Crawford Agroforestry Research Trust course at his plot in Devon, bringing back ideas and suitable plants for our soil. The plot was sown with alder trees, and fruit and nut trees, and a mate dug us a pair of ponds. Just recently, Pat's son, Scott, has taken a greater interest in the plot, and is turning it into a market garden/allotment with a vast array of vegetables, working towards self-sufficiency. An old Highway Board workman's hut provides shelter, and a generator provides us with heat and light. We go there about four times a week to generally chill out: Otis loves galloping through the meadow, so many sights and smells for him!

REGRETS
Not many. A 90mph Manx lap would have been nice (seven seconds too long); and I would have quite fancied a go at ice speedway, by myself, without a burly Russian, Vladimir Knockemoff or Ivan Kickemoff, trying to ride up my inside leg.

POSTSCRIPT: AUGUST 2020
The Island locked its borders when Covid arrived; we had at least 70 Covid-free days, and then I copped a slight heart attack – bugger! I'm glad to say that, due to the excellent service I received from the CCU unit at Nobles Hospital, I am feeling back to my 'short-portly' self again. I managed to lose about 10 per cent of my body weight during lockdown, from 100kg to below 90kg!

In our supposed dotage, there is nothing nicer than sitting on Laxey Prom, with one of Julie's fabulous Cornish recipe ice creams, or her signature pork bap with stuffing. The vista is spectacular, even in rough weather with the Irish Sea pounding in, no high-rise to blight the view, at peace with the world. Or sitting in JJ Ribbons, putting the world to rights, with the trams shuffling past, and the distant view of the Great Laxey Wheel, The Lady Isabella slowly turning. Heaven!

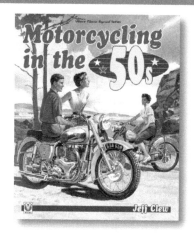

For those who were there, and for those fascinated by 1950s British culture, Jeff Clew's insight to motorcycling in the '50s will provide a delightful nostalgic journey into the past, while those younger riders who cherish 1950s motorcycles today will discover a whole new dimension to their enjoyment of the machines.

ISBN: 978-1-787110-99-1
Paperback • 25x20.7cm • 144 pages

An inside look behind the scenes at the top-secret planning, build-up, and spectacular success of Mike Hailwood's amazing comeback in 1978, 20 years after his debut at the age of 18. Written by his manager and friend, Ted Macauley, it is also a tribute to a remarkable man.

ISBN: 978-1-787113-13-8
Paperback • 21x14.8cm • 112 pages

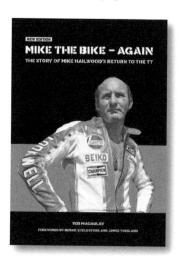

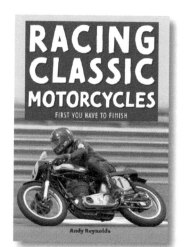

The life of a classic motorcycle racer, who was fortunate enough to ride the best classic machines between 1976 & 2016 at the highest level, and on some of the best-known courses in the world. Told in his own words, this book recounts his successes, friendships, and hardships, and gives great insight into the world of motorcycle racing.

ISBN: 978-1-787114-81-4
Paperback • 21x14.8cm • 240 pages

For more information and price details, visit **www.veloce.co.uk**
• email: info@veloce.co.uk • Tel: +44(0)1305 260068

Index